SCHOLASTIC

2014 BOOK OF WORLD RECORDS

by Jenifer Corr Morse
A GEORGIAN BAY BOOK

SCHOLASTIC INC.

To Isabelle Nicole—May you always find wonder in the world.
—JCM

CREATED AND PRODUCED BY GEORGIAN BAY LLC
Copyright © 2013 by Georgian Bay LLC

GEORGIAN BAY STAFF
Bruce S. Glassman, Executive Editor
Jenifer Corr Morse, Author
Joe Bernier, Designer

ISBN 978-0-545-56262-1

10 9 8 7 6 5 4 3 2 1   13 14 15 16 17

Printed in the U.S.A.   40
First edition, November 2013

Cover design by Kay Petronio
Deb Cohn-Orbach, Photo Editor

In most cases, the graphs in this book represent the top five record holders in each category. However, in some graphs, we have chosen to list well-known or common people, places, animals, or things that will help you better understand how extraordinary the record holder is. These may not be the top five in the category. Additionally, some graphs have fewer than five entries because so few people or objects reflect the necessary criteria.

Due to the publication date, the majority of statistics is current as of May 2013.

Contents

Science & Technology Records

video games
internet
technology
vehicles
structures
transportation
environment

Talk Time?

What are people doing when they're scrolling on their cell phones? About 61 percent are playing games, 55 percent are checking the weather, and 49 percent are using social networks. In fact, people spend about 2.7 hours a day socializing on their cells—more than twice the time they spend eating and about a third of the time they spend sleeping.

Sweet Tweets

There have been more than 163 billion tweets since Twitter began in 2006. The United States has the most Twitter accounts with more than 140 million. However, the top three tweeting cities are Jakarta, Tokyo, and London. The average user has tweeted 307 times.

Lots to Say

About 3 million new blogs come online each month. About 60 percent of bloggers are between 25 and 44 years old, and 20 percent of bloggers have been doing it for more than 6 years. Professional bloggers maintain an average of 4 blogs at a time.

Picture This

Instagram is taking social media by storm with about 575 likes per second. More than 5 million photos are uploaded every day. Instagram started in 2012, and it has 100 million active monthly users. Users spend about 257 minutes using Instagram each month.

Rise Hudson Valencia

Standing Tall

The tallest indoor statue in the United States is located in the Parthenon in Nashville, Tennessee's Centennial Park. The 42-foot (12.8-m) statue of Athena is an exact replica of the original in ancient Greece's Parthenon. Alan LeQuire began creating the 4-story statue in 1982, and it was originally all white. In 2002, the statue was coated in gold to more closely resemble the original.

Hold on Tight!

The Smiler, which opened in May 2013 at Alton Towers Resort in the UK, is the first roller coaster in the world to have 14 inversions. The ride has a top speed of 52.8 miles (85 km) per hour, and lasts about 165 seconds. The track that creates the 14 loops measures 3,838 feet (1170 m) and weighs about 771 tons (700 t).

Up, Up, and Away

The longest airplane flight travels from Johannesburg, South Africa, to Atlanta, Georgia, and lasts for 17 hours. The longest flight route is between Sydney, Australia, and Dallas, Texas—it stretches for about 8,500 miles (13,679 km). At any one time, there are about 61,000 people in flight above the United States.

bestselling video game

Pokémon Black/White, Version 2

The second version of Pokémon Black/White sold more than 6 million copies in 2012. This version picks up in Unova two years after the original game ended. The journey begins in Aspertia City, and players meet many new characters, as well as some old favorites, along the way. There are also some new regions to explore. Players can solve the mystery of Kyurem—a special Pokémon dragon with an ice attack. There are more than 150 new Pokémon, and players can participate in battles with two other monsters at the same time. Nintendo released Pokémon Black/White Version 2 in March 2011, and it has sold more than 15 million copies since.

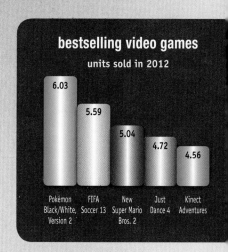

bestselling video games

units sold in 2012

6.03	5.59	5.04	4.72	4.56
Pokémon Black/White, Version 2	FIFA Soccer 13	New Super Mario Bros. 2	Just Dance 4	Kinect Adventures

bestselling video console

3DS

The most popular gaming console in 2012 was Nintendo 3DS, selling almost 14 million units. Gamers can enjoy all the 3-D effects without glasses. The console has two screens, and its 3-D technology supports movies and videos. It also features three cameras, an activity log, an Internet browser, and access to the Nintendo Network. When it was first released in February 2011, 3DS had the highest one-day sales of any Nintendo portable gaming device. During the first week of release, about 440,000 units were sold.

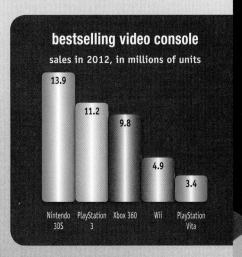

bestselling video console
sales in 2012, in millions of units

Nintendo 3DS	PlayStation 3	Xbox 360	Wii	PlayStation Vita
13.9	11.2	9.8	4.9	3.4

bestselling video game franchise

Super Mario

With lifetime sales of more than 290 million copies, Super Mario is the bestselling video game franchise in history. Since the series launched in the United States in 1985, there have been many successful games in the franchise, including Super Mario Bros. (40.2 million), New Super Mario Bros. (53 million), Super Mario World (20.6 million), and Super Mario Land (18.1 million). The games' heroes, Mario and Luigi, originally raced through Mushroom Kingdom to save Princess Toadstool. As the series has expanded, these heroes have driven racecars, traveled to different lands, and even left the galaxy.

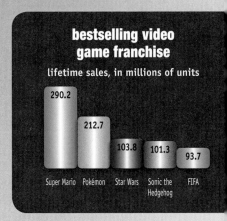

bestselling video game franchise

lifetime sales, in millions of units

Super Mario	Pokémon	Star Wars	Sonic the Hedgehog	FIFA
290.2	212.7	103.8	101.3	93.7

most-visited social site

Facebook

More than 750 million unique visitors click on the Facebook website each month. That's more than the next four social sites combined. Facebook was founded by Mark Zuckerberg in 2004 as a way for Harvard students to keep in touch. Ten years later, Facebook has more than 1 billion registered users, and about 552 million log on every day. Every minute of the day, about 684,478 pieces of content are shared. People spend an average of 6.75 hours on Facebook each month. There are around 140 billion friend connections, and 500 million "likes" per day.

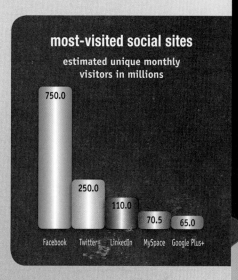

most-visited social sites

estimated unique monthly visitors in millions

Facebook	Twitter	LinkedIn	MySpace	Google Plus+
750.0	250.0	110.0	70.5	65.0

most-used search engine

Google

About 67 percent of people browsing the Internet choose Google as their search engine. Google is the world's largest online index of websites. In addition, Google offers e-mail, maps, news, and financial services. Headquartered in California's Silicon Valley, the company runs hundreds of thousands of servers around the globe. A "googol" is a 1 followed by 100 zeros, and the site was named after the term to indicate its mission to organize the virtually infinite amount of information on the web.

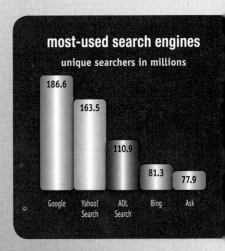

most-used search engines

unique searchers in millions

Google	Yahoo! Search	AOL Search	Bing	Ask
186.6	163.5	110.9	81.3	77.9

most-visited website

Google

The most-visited website in the world is Google, which gets more than 186 million unique page views per month. Created by Stanford grad students Larry Page and Sergey Brin in 1998, Google has indexed 30 trillion pages. Google performs about 100 billion searches each month. There are more than 425 million people using Gmail, the website's e-mail feature. Over the years, Google has acquired many impressive companies, including YouTube, Android, DoubleClick, and Blogger. Google employs more than 50,000 people worldwide.

most-visited websites

unique visitors per month

Google	Microsoft sites	Yahoo!	Facebook	YouTube
186.6	166.7	163.5	152.2	136.0

most-visited shopping site

Amazon.com

Shopping megasite Amazon.com had $48 billion in sales in 2012. The site, which got its start selling books, now offers everything from clothes and electronics to food and furniture. Founded by Jeffrey Bezos in 1994, it is headquartered in Seattle, Washington. The company also has separate websites in countries including Japan, Canada, the United Kingdom, Germany, and France.

most-visited shopping sites
online sales, in billions of US dollars

Amazon	Staples	Apple	Walmart	Dell
48.0	10.6	6.6	4.9	4.6

most-viewed YouTube account in 2012

Universal Music Group

The Universal Music Group's videos were seen on YouTube more than 5.89 billion times in 2012. A giant in the music world, the company owns all or part of many of the country's hottest labels, including Interscope-Geffen-A&M, Def Jam Music Group, Republic Records, and Capitol Music Group. All of these labels include hundreds of artists, and some of today's biggest stars, such as The Black Eyed Peas, Justin Bieber, Jennifer Lopez, Nicki Minaj, Rihanna, and many others. Some of the most popular videos include "We Are Never Ever Getting Back Together," by Taylor Swift, and "Diamonds," by Rihanna.

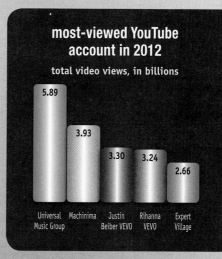

most-viewed YouTube account in 2012

total video views, in billions

5.89	3.93	3.30	3.24	2.66
Universal Music Group	Machinima	Justin Beiber VEVO	Rihanna VEVO	Expert Village

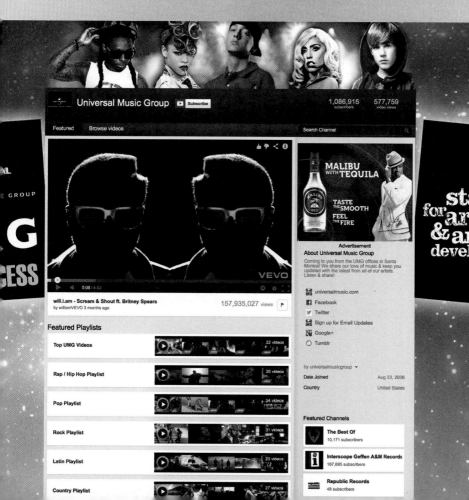

most-viewed YouTube video

"Gangnam Style"

South Korean singer PSY released "Gangnam Style" in July 2012, and it has since become the most-viewed video on YouTube with more than 1 billion hits. In fact, it had more than 500,000 views on its first day. In December 2012, it averaged about 76.4 views per second. It was the first single off his sixth album, *PSY 6 (Six Rules), Part 1*. The song, which debuted at the top of the South Korean charts, describes the trendy lifestyle of the Gangnam region in Seoul. "Gangnam Style" won Best Video at the South Korea 2012 MTV Video Music Awards.

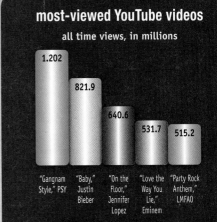

most-viewed YouTube videos
all time views, in millions

"Gangnam Style," PSY	"Baby," Justin Bieber	"On the Floor," Jennifer Lopez	"Love the Way You Lie," Eminem	"Party Rock Anthem," LMFAO
1,202	821.9	640.6	531.7	515.2

most popular facebook games

CityVille/Words with Friends

Every day, the popular Facebook games CityVille and Words with Friends are each played by about 7.8 million gamers worldwide. CityVille was created by Zynga, and lets players build the cities of their dreams by opening franchises, collecting rent, and even arresting criminals. Words with Friends, also created by Zynga, is a game in which players take turns scoring points from the words they create with letter tiles that have been randomly assigned. Both CityVille and Words with Friends can be played with other online friends.

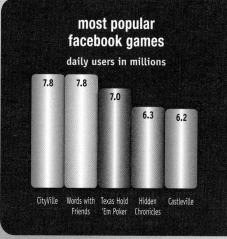

most popular facebook games

daily users in millions

CityVille	Words with Friends	Texas Hold 'Em Poker	Hidden Chronicles	Castleville
7.8	7.8	7.0	6.3	6.2

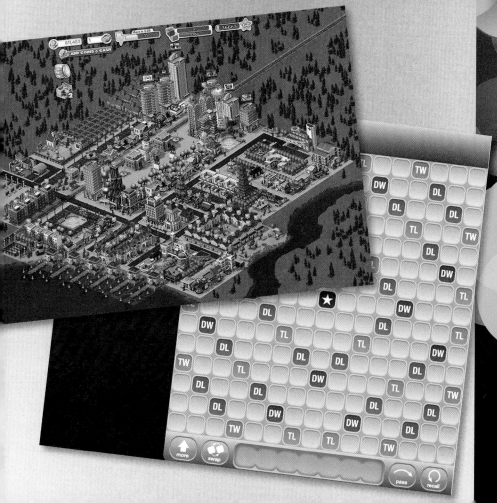

product with the
most facebook fans

Coca-Cola

Coca-Cola is the most popular product on Facebook with 56 million fans. On the page, fans can post and read stories, explore products, and check out the latest photos. The company has acquired some impressive statistics during its 128 years in business. Coca-Cola produces more than 3,500 different types of beverages, which are sold in 200 countries throughout the world. Each day, about 1.7 billion servings of Coca-Cola products are enjoyed. In addition to its cola products, the company also produces A&W, Crush, Dasani, Hi-C, Minute Maid, Nestea, and many others.

products with the most facebook fans

number of fans, in millions

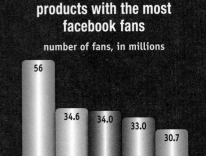

Coca-Cola	Red Bull	Converse All Stars	Starbucks	Oreo
56	34.6	34.0	33.0	30.7

most-searched image on google

One Direction

Fans love to see the guys of One Direction, and the group became the most-searched image on Google in 2012. The five-man English band, which is made up of Niall Horan, Zayn Malik, Liam Payne, Harry Styles, and Louis Tomlinson, were finalists on *The X-Factor* (U.K.) in 2010. They finished third on the reality show, but were signed by Simon Cowell's Syco Records that year. They later signed with Columbia Records, and have released two albums—*Up All Night* and *Take Me Home*. Google images was created in July 2001, and currently has more than 10 billion items indexed.

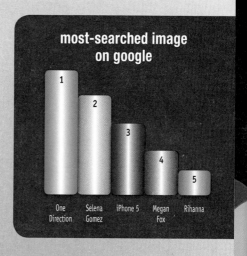

most-searched image on google

1. One Direction
2. Selena Gomez
3. iPhone 5
4. Megan Fox
5. Rihanna

YouTube

Search

Animals That Do Exist

stevefowler 8 videos ⌄ Subscribe

AP / Gautam Singh

‖ ◁› 1:00 / 2:32   360p ♫

👍 Like   👎   + Add to ▾   Share   ▤   **4,633,45**

Uploaded by stevefowler on Jul 12, 2007   2,492 likes, 1,172 dislike

They do

Show more ⌄

most-visited video site

YouTube

When web surfers are looking for videos, the majority log on to YouTube. With more than 136 million unique visitors per month, YouTube can turn everyday people into Internet stars. On the site, anyone can upload their own videos for the world to see. YouTube gets about 3 billion views per day. Each minute, about 48 hours of video is uploaded to the site. In fact, more video is uploaded to YouTube in one month than the three largest broadcast networks could create in 60 years. About 500 years' worth of YouTube video is shared on Facebook each day, and another 700 YouTube videos are shared on Twitter each minute.

most-visited video sites

unique visitors per month, in millions

YouTube	136.0
Yahoo!	43.3
Vevo	42
AOL Media Network	25.5
MSN/Windows/Bing	24.3

country with the most twitter accounts

USA

There are more than 141.5 million Twitter accounts in the United States. That's more than the next four top countries combined! In total, Twitter has 465 million accounts. Each day, about 1 million new Twitter accounts are opened—an average of 11.5 accounts per second. In just one week, approximately 1.2 billion tweets are sent out. About 40 percent of all users don't even tweet—they just follow others. And about half of all Twitter users access their accounts on their cell phones. Twitter was created in July 2006 by Jack Dorsey, Biz Stone, and Evan Williams.

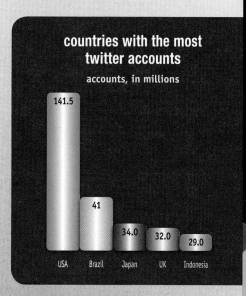

countries with the most twitter accounts

accounts, in millions

USA	Brazil	Japan	UK	Indonesia
141.5	41	34.0	32.0	29.0

Twitter / Home - Windows Internet Expl

https://twitter.com/home

Twitter / Home

twitter

What are you doing?

Waiting for my train to

celebrity with the most twitter followers

Justin Bieber

Justin Bieber's fans will follow him anywhere, including on social media. With 39.3 million followers, Bieber is the king of Twitter. While some analysis suggests that a portion of his followers—along with other top celebrities on Twitter—are from spam accounts, this cannot be proven. "Beliebers" around the world have been obsessed with the Canadian pop star since his debut in 2009. In the last five years, he has sold more than 12 million albums, and his breakout hit, "Baby," has been viewed more than 750 million times on YouTube. He's even had great success selling all kinds of products including greeting cards, fragrances, and toothbrushes.

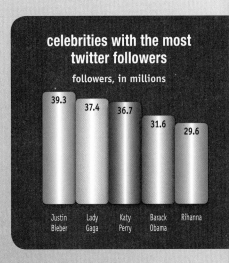

celebrities with the most twitter followers

followers, in millions

Justin Bieber	Lady Gaga	Katy Perry	Barack Obama	Rihanna
39.3	37.4	36.7	31.6	29.6

most active twitter moment

Castle in the Sky airing

The annual television screening of the 27-year-old animated Japanese film classic *Castle in the Sky* averaged 25,088 tweets per second! When *Castle in the Sky* aired in December 2011 in Japan, fans were encouraged to tweet the word "balse" to help Pazu and Sheeta—the main characters—cast a spell. Clearly fans responded. The film was created in Japan by Hayao Miyazaki and was released in 1986. It was later rereleased in English by Disney in 1999. The English version featured the voices of James Van Der Beek, Anna Paquin, Cloris Leachman, and Mark Hamill.

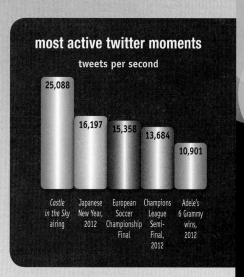

most active twitter moments

tweets per second

Castle in the Sky airing	Japanese New Year, 2012	European Soccer Championship Final	Champions League Semi-Final, 2012	Adele's 6 Grammy wins, 2012
25,088	16,197	15,358	13,684	10,901

country with the highest internet usage

Iceland

Iceland has the world's highest percentage of Internet users, with more than 97.8 percent of the country logging on to surf the web. That means about 302,000 people in the small European country have Internet access, and 98,000 are broadband subscribers. In comparison, only about 34 percent of the world's population in the rest of Europe goes online. Icelandic people mainly use the Internet to find information and to communicate, with about 45 percent of users also shopping online.

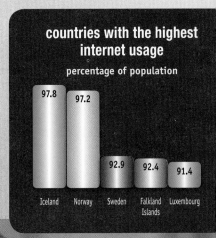

countries with the highest internet usage
percentage of population

Iceland	Norway	Sweden	Falkland Islands	Luxembourg
97.8	97.2	92.9	92.4	91.4

country with the most internet users

China

China dominates the world in Internet usage, with 538 million people—or about one-third of the country—browsing the World Wide Web under government censorship. The number of Internet users in China has tripled in the last five years. About 250 million Internet users browse from their cell phones. These phone-surfers account for much of the increase in Internet users. People spend an average of almost 20 hours a week online. Some Internet activities that are becoming increasingly popular in China include banking and booking travel.

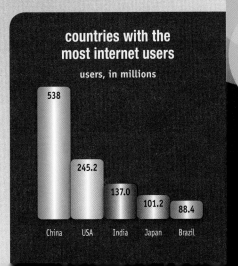

countries with the most internet users

users, in millions

China	USA	India	Japan	Brazil
538	245.2	137.0	101.2	88.4

25

bestselling cell phone brand

Nokia

Nokia is the most popular cell phone brand worldwide. It accounted for 23.8 percent of the market share—or total number of people buying cell phones—in 2012. Since launching its first mobile phone in 1992, the Finnish company has sold 460 million phones in 150 countries. Nokia introduced its first 3G phone in 2003, and went on to sell its 1 billionth phone in 2005. In 2007, Nokia's N95 became the first phone to combine GPS service and wireless broadband. The company operates 15 manufacturing plants across the globe and employs 123,000 people.

bestselling cell phone brands

percentage of market share

Nokia	Samsung	Apple	LG Electronics	ZTE
23.8	17.7	5.0	4.9	3.2

united states' bestselling smartphones

Android

The Android maintains the lead in the American smartphone race, with 51.7 percent of the market share. They are most popular with buyers ages 18 to 34, and men slightly outnumber women in ownership rates. On average, Android users have 22 apps. The top four apps on the Android are Google Maps, Facebook, the Weather Channel, and Pandora. And users remain loyal—more than 70 percent of current Android users intend to buy another when it comes time. About 57 percent of US cell phone users now own a smartphone.

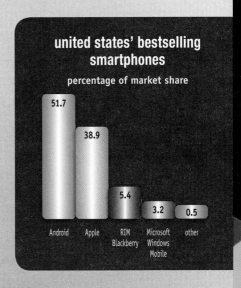

united states' bestselling smartphones
percentage of market share

Android	Apple	RIM Blackberry	Microsoft Windows Mobile	other
51.7	38.9	5.4	3.2	0.5

most popular mobile app

Facebook

Smartphone users check their Facebook apps most, with 85.5 million unique users each month. Facebook also dominates a smartphone user's mobile time, accounting for 23 percent of the time the user is checking apps. That's more than the next six most popular apps combined. While browsing their Facebook apps, users can post and check status updates, share and view photos, and read and send private messages. Facebook has more than 1 billion users.

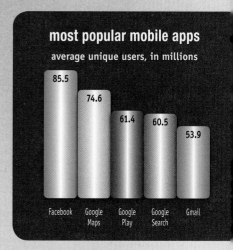

most popular mobile apps
average unique users, in millions

Facebook	Google Maps	Google Play	Google Search	Gmail
85.5	74.6	61.4	60.5	53.9

bestselling app type

Games

Games are the top app choice among smartphone users, with about 43 percent of users downloading them. Some of the bestselling iPhone games include Rayman Jungle Run, Letterpress, and Angry Birds Space. Some of the most popular Android games include Temple Run: 02, Need for Speed Most Wanted, and Angry Birds Space Premium. More than 25 percent of adults download apps regularly, and the average user has about 18 of them. More than 300,000 mobile apps have been developed in the last three years, and a total of 10.9 billion have been downloaded.

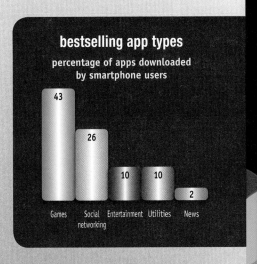

bestselling app types

percentage of apps downloaded by smartphone users

Games	Social networking	Entertainment	Utilities	News
43	26	10	10	2

bestselling e-reader

Amazon Kindle

Amazon's Kindle dominates the market, accounting for almost half of all e-reader sales. The Kindle, which is a book-sized device onto which owners can download their favorite reading material, lets readers shop for, and read, books, magazines, and newspapers all in one spot. Some titles can be "loaned" to another Kindle user. The device also comes with a free electronic dictionary so users can look up unknown words as they read. The first Kindle was released in November 2007, but now comes in several models, including the original, Fire, Fire HD, and Paperwhite.

bestselling e-reader

percentage of the market

48.0	20.6	18.6	16.9	9.4
Amazon Kindle	Other	Pandigital	B&N Nook	Sony

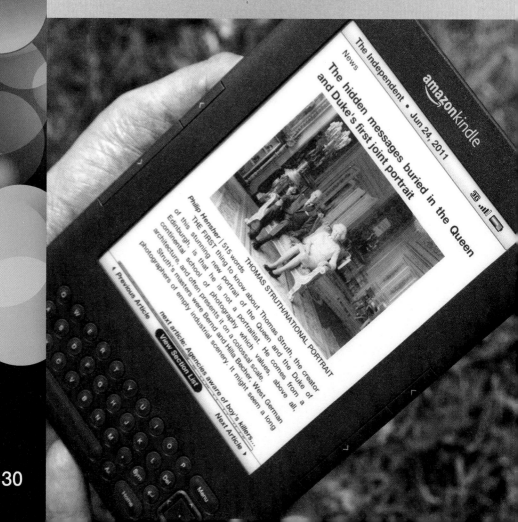

country that watches the most tv

United States

The United States likes to watch a lot of television, averaging 33 hours of weekly program viewing per household. That's the equivalent of more than 71 straight days, or 2 months per year. People ages 65 and older watch the most at 48 hours per week, while teens watch the least at 22 hours. Ninety-eight percent of American households own at least one television, and about 54 percent of children have a set in their bedrooms. About 6 percent of families watch TV while eating dinner, and about 70 percent of day-care centers use televisions as well.

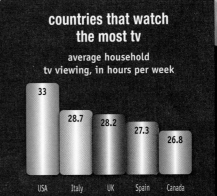

countries that watch the most tv

average household
tv viewing, in hours per week

USA	Italy	UK	Spain	Canada
33	28.7	28.2	27.3	26.8

largest cruise ships

Oasis of the Seas & Allure of the Seas

Royal Caribbean's sister cruise ships—*Oasis of the Seas* and *Allure of the Seas*—weigh in at 225,282 gross tons (228,897 t) each! These giant ships are more like floating cities with seven different themed neighborhoods: Central Park, Boardwalk, Royal Promenade, Pool and Sports Zone, Vitality at Sea Spa and Fitness Center, Entertainment Place, and Youth Zone. *Oasis of the Seas* and *Allure of the Seas* each feature 16 decks and include more than 20 eateries, 3 pools, a water park, and a zip-line ride. Both ships have 2,700 staterooms and can accommodate a whopping 5,400 guests.

largest cruise ships

weight, in gross tons (tonnes)

Oasis of the Seas	Allure of the Seas	Independence of the Seas	Liberty of the Seas	Freedom of the Seas
225,282 (228,897)	225,282 (228,897)	160,000 (162,567)	160,000 (162,567)	160,000 (162,567)

Oasis of the Seas

fastest passenger train

CRH380AL

When China unveiled the CRH380AL commercial passenger train in 2010, it cruised into the record books with a top speed of 302 miles (486 km) per hour. The train reached its top speed in just 22 minutes. Its lightweight aluminum body and streamlined head help the CRH380AL travel that fast. The train's route connects Beijing and Shanghai, and reduced the average travel time from 10 hours to 4 hours. The train is part of China's $313 billion program to develop the world's most advanced train system by 2020.

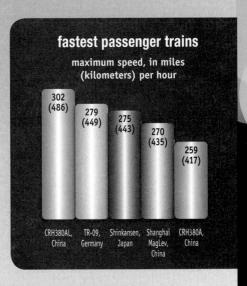

fastest passenger trains

maximum speed, in miles (kilometers) per hour

CRH380AL, China	302 (486)
TR-09, Germany	279 (449)
Shinkansen, Japan	275 (443)
Shanghai MagLev, China	270 (435)
CRH380A, China	259 (417)

biggest monster truck

Bigfoot 5

The Bigfoot 5 truly is a monster—it measures 15.4 feet (4.7 m) high! That's about three times the height of an average car. Bigfoot 5 has 10-foot (3 m) Firestone Tundra tires, each weighing 2,400 pounds (1,088 kg), giving the truck a total weight of about 38,000 pounds (17,236 kg). The giant wheels were from an arctic snow train operated in Alaska by the US Army in the 1950s. This modified 1996 Ford F250 pickup truck is owned by Bob Chandler of St. Louis, Missouri. The great weight of this monster truck makes it too large to race.

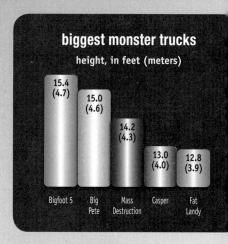

biggest monster trucks
height, in feet (meters)

Bigfoot 5	Big Pete	Mass Destruction	Casper	Fat Landy
15.4 (4.7)	15.0 (4.6)	14.2 (4.3)	13.0 (4.0)	12.8 (3.9)

smallest car

Peel P50

The Peel P50 is the smallest production car ever made, measuring just 4.5 feet (1.4 m) long. That's not much longer than the average adult bicycle! The Peel P50 was originally produced in the Isle of Man between 1962 and 1965, and only 46 cars were made. However, the company began production again in 2012. The Peel P50 has three wheels, one door, one windshield wiper, and one headlight. The microcar weighs just 130 pounds (58.9 kg) and measures about 4 feet (1.2 m) tall. With its three-speed manual transmission, it can reach a top speed of 38 miles (61 km) an hour. It cannot, however, go in reverse.

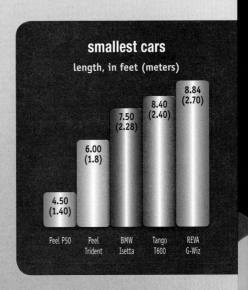

smallest cars
length, in feet (meters)

Peel P50	Peel Trident	BMW Isetta	Tango T600	REVA G-Wiz
4.50 (1.40)	6.00 (1.8)	7.50 (2.28)	8.40 (2.40)	8.84 (2.70)

fastest land vehicle

Thrust SSC

The Thrust SSC, which stands for Supersonic Car, reached a speed of 763 miles (1,228 km) per hour on October 15, 1997. At that speed, a car could make it from San Francisco to New York City in less than four hours. The Thrust SSC is propelled by two jet engines capable of 110,000 horsepower. It has the same power as 1,000 Ford Escorts or 145 Formula One race cars. The Thrust SSC runs on jet fuel, using about 5 gallons (19 L) per second. It takes only approximately five seconds for this supersonic car to reach its top speed. It is 54 feet (16.5 m) long and weighs 7 tons (6.4 t).

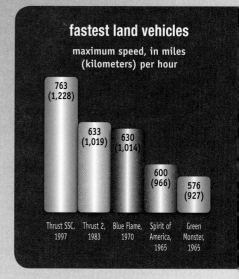

fastest land vehicles

maximum speed, in miles (kilometers) per hour

763 (1,228)	633 (1,019)	630 (1,014)	600 (966)	576 (927)
Thrust SSC, 1997	Thrust 2, 1983	Blue Flame, 1970	Spirit of America, 1965	Green Monster, 1965

fastest production motorcycle

MTT Turbine Superbike Y2K

The MTT Turbine Superbike Y2K—the first turbine-powered, street-legal motorcycle—hits a top speed of 230 miles (370 km/h) per hour, or about 3.5 times the speed on an average highway. A Rolls-Royce Allison gas turbine engine powers the bike, and its aluminum alloy frame and carbon fiber fairings keep the weight down. The MTT Turbine Superbike also features a two-speed automatic transmission, Pirelli tires, and Brembo brakes, and comes in any color the buyer can imagine. The bike retails for about $175,000.

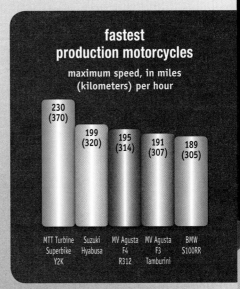

fastest production motorcycles

maximum speed, in miles (kilometers) per hour

MTT Turbine Superbike Y2K	Suzuki Hyabusa	MV Agusta F4 R312	MV Agusta F3 Tamburini	BMW S100RR
230 (370)	199 (320)	195 (314)	191 (307)	189 (305)

Bugatti Veyron 16.4 Super Sport

With a top cruising speed of 268 miles (431 km) per hour, the Bugatti Veyron 16.4 Super Sport is the fastest production car in the world. It can cruise at more than four times the average speed limit on most highways! The Super Sport has a sleek, aerodynamic design that feeds air to the 16-cylinder engine from the roof, rather than just above the hood. The shell of the car is made of carbon-fiber composites to make the car lighter, while maintaining its safety. The Super Sport debuted at the Pebble Beach Concourse in August 2010.

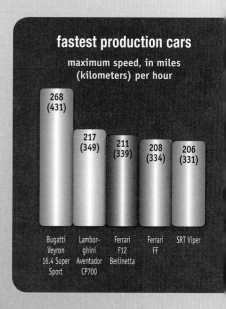

fastest production cars

maximum speed, in miles (kilometers) per hour

Bugatti Veyron 16.4 Super Sport	Lamborghini Aventador CP700	Ferrari F12 Berlinetta	Ferrari FF	SRT Viper
268 (431)	217 (349)	211 (339)	208 (334)	206 (331)

fastest traditional helicopter

Sikorsky X-2

The Sikorsky X-2 experimental compound helicopter reached a top speed of 287 miles (462 km) per hour in September 2010. The successful flight lasted just over one hour. Sikorsky was able to accomplish this record-breaking speed in 17 test flights with just over 16 flight hours. The company made several improvements to the original X-2—including reducing the drag, implementing rigid rotor blades, and finalizing vibration control—to achieve its success. Sikorsky continues to experiment with the X-2 to increase speed and performance for future models to be used by the military.

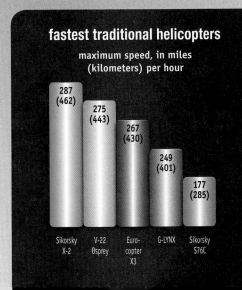

fastest traditional helicopters

maximum speed, in miles (kilometers) per hour

Sikorsky X-2	V-22 Osprey	Euro-copter X3	G-LYNX	Sikorsky S76C
287 (462)	275 (443)	267 (430)	249 (401)	177 (285)

lightest jet

BD-5J Microjet

The BD-5J Microjet weighs only 358.8 pounds (162.7 kg), making it the lightest jet in the world. At only 12 feet (3.7 m) in length, it is one of the smallest as well. This tiny jet has a height of 5.6 feet (1.7 m) and a wingspan of 17 feet (5.2 m). The Microjet uses a TRS-18 turbojet engine. It can reach a top speed of 320 miles (514.9 km) per hour, but can carry only 32 gallons (121 L) of fuel at a time. A new BD-5J costs around $200,000. This high-tech gadget was flown by James Bond in the movie *Octopussy*, and it is also occasionally used by the US military.

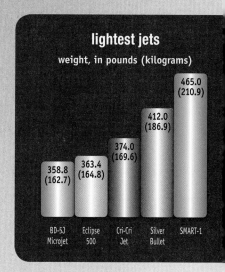

lightest jets
weight, in pounds (kilograms)

				465.0 (210.9)
			412.0 (186.9)	
		374.0 (169.6)		
358.8 (162.7)	363.4 (164.8)			
BD-5J Microjet	Eclipse 500	Cri-Cri Jet	Silver Bullet	SMART-1

fastest plane

X-43A

NASA's experimental X-43A plane reached a top speed of Mach 9.8—or more than nine times the speed of sound—on a test flight over the Pacific Ocean in November 2004. The X-43A was mounted on top of a Pegasus rocket booster and was carried into the sky by a B-52 aircraft. The booster was then fired, taking the X-43A about 110,000 feet (33,530 m) above the ground. The rocket was detached from the unmanned X-43A, and the plane flew unassisted for several minutes. At this rate of 7,459 miles (12,004 km) per hour, a plane could circle Earth in just over three and a half hours!

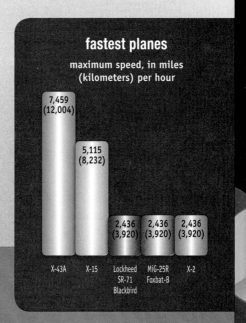

fastest planes

maximum speed, in miles (kilometers) per hour

Plane	Speed
X-43A	7,459 (12,004)
X-15	5,115 (8,232)
Lockheed SR-71 Blackbird	2,436 (3,920)
MiG-25R Foxbat-B	2,436 (3,920)
X-2	2,436 (3,920)

tallest roller coaster

Kingda Ka

Kingda Ka towers over Six Flags Great Adventure in Jackson, New Jersey, at a height of 456 feet (139 m). Its highest drop plummets riders down 418 feet (127 m). The steel coaster can reach a top speed of 128 miles (206 km) per hour in just 3.5 seconds, and it was the fastest coaster in the world when it opened in 2005. The entire 3,118-foot (950 m) ride is over in just 28 seconds. The hydraulic launch coaster is located in the Golden Kingdom section of the park. It can accommodate about 1,400 riders per hour.

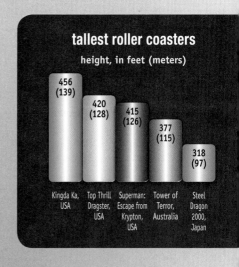

tallest roller coasters
height, in feet (meters)

Kingda Ka, USA	Top Thrill Dragster, USA	Superman: Escape from Krypton, USA	Tower of Terror, Australia	Steel Dragon 2000, Japan
456 (139)	420 (128)	415 (126)	377 (115)	318 (97)

amusement park with the most rides

Cedar Point

Located in Sandusky, Ohio, Cedar Point offers park visitors 74 rides to enjoy. GateKeeper—the park's newest ride—is the fastest and longest-running winged roller coaster in the world. Top Thrill Dragster roller coaster is the second tallest in the world at 420 feet (128 m). And with 17 roller coasters, Cedar Point also has the most coasters of any theme park in the world. Over 53,963 feet (16,448 m) of coaster track—more than 10 miles (16.1 km)—run through the park. Cedar Point has been named Best Amusement Park in the World by *Amusement Today* for the past 15 years.

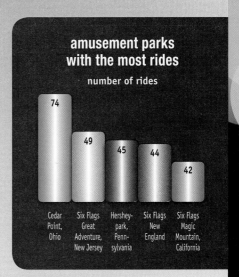

amusement parks with the most rides

number of rides

Cedar Point, Ohio	Six Flags Great Adventure, New Jersey	Hershey-park, Penn-sylvania	Six Flags New England	Six Flags Magic Mountain, California
74	49	45	44	42

43

fastest roller coaster

Formula Rossa

The Formula Rossa coaster in the United Arab Emirates speeds past the competition with a top speed of 149 miles (240 km) per hour. Located at Ferrari World in Dubai, riders climb into the F1 race car cockpits and can experience what 4.8 g-force actually feels like. The coaster's hydraulic launch system rockets the coaster to its top speed in just 4.9 seconds. The track is about 1.4 miles (2.2 km) long, with the sharpest turn measuring 70 degrees. To protect riders' eyes from flying insects, safety goggles must be worn throughout the ride.

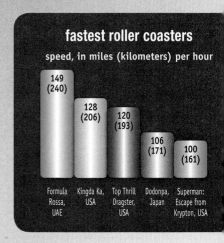

fastest roller coasters

speed, in miles (kilometers) per hour

149 (240)				
	128 (206)			
		120 (193)		
			106 (171)	100 (161)
Formula Rossa, UAE	Kingda Ka, USA	Top Thrill Dragster, USA	Dodonpa, Japan	Superman: Escape from Krypton, USA

city with the most skyscrapers

New York

New York City has the most skyscrapers in the world with 212 buildings that reach 500 feet (152 m) or higher. The three tallest buildings in the Big Apple are One World Trade Center at 1,776 feet (541 m), the Empire State Building at 1,250 feet (381 m), and the Bank of America Tower at 1,200 feet (366 m). One World Trade Center is the tallest building in the Western Hemisphere. The first skyscrapers popped up in New York City in the mid-1890s. With more than 22.1 million people currently living in the metropolitan area, architects have to continue building up instead of out.

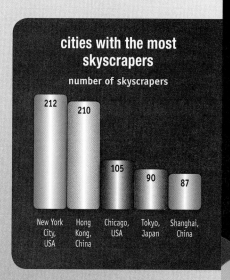

cities with the most skyscrapers

number of skyscrapers

New York City, USA	Hong Kong, China	Chicago, USA	Tokyo, Japan	Shanghai, China
212	210	105	90	87

tallest habitable building

Burj Khalifa

Burj Khalifa in the United Arab Emirates towers 2,717 feet (828 m) above the ground. With more than 160 floors, the building cost about $4.1 billion to construct. Both a hotel and apartments are housed inside the luxury building, which covers 500 acres (202 ha). The building features high-speed elevators that travel at 40 miles (64 km) per hour. The tower supplies its occupants with about 250,000 gallons (66,043 l) of water a day, and delivers enough electricity to power 360,000 100-watt lightbulbs.

tallest habitable buildings

height, in feet (meters)

Burj Khalifa, UAE	Makkah Clock Royal Tower, Saudi Arabia	Taipei 101, Taiwan	Shanghai World Financial Center, China	International Commerce Centre, Hong Kong
2,717 (828)	1,971 (601)	1,671 (509)	1,614 (492)	1,588 (484)

largest swimming pool

San Alfonso Del Mar

The gigantic swimming pool at the San Alfonso del Mar resort, in Chile, spreads over 19.7 acres (8 ha). The monstrous pool is the equivalent to 6,000 standard swimming pools and holds 66 million gallons (250 million L) of water. In addition to swimming, guests can sail and scuba dive in the saltwater lagoon, which is surrounded by white sand beaches. And there's no diving for pennies here—the deep end measures 115 feet (35 m). The pool took five years to complete and first opened in December 2006. The project cost $2 billion, and costs about $4 million annually to maintain it.

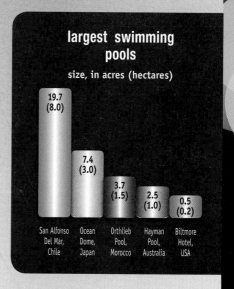

largest swimming pools

size, in acres (hectares)

San Alfonso Del Mar, Chile	Ocean Dome, Japan	Orthlieb Pool, Morocco	Hayman Pool, Australia	Biltmore Hotel, USA
19.7 (8.0)	7.4 (3.0)	3.7 (1.5)	2.5 (1.0)	0.5 (0.2)

47

largest sports stadium

Rungrado May First Stadium

The Rungrado May First Stadium, also known as the May Day Stadium, can seat up to 150,000 people. The interior of the stadium covers 2.2 million square feet (204,386 sq m). Located in Pyongyang, North Korea, this venue is mostly used for soccer matches and other athletic contests. It is named after Rungra Island, on which the stadium is located, in the middle of the Taedong River. When it is not being used for sporting events, the stadium is used for a two-month festival known as Arirang.

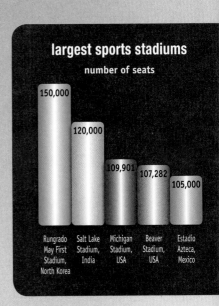

largest sports stadiums
number of seats

150,000	120,000	109,901	107,282	105,000
Rungrado May First Stadium, North Korea	Salt Lake Stadium, India	Michigan Stadium, USA	Beaver Stadium, USA	Estadio Azteca, Mexico

busiest airport

Hartsfield-Jackson Atlanta International Airport

The Hartsfield-Jackson Atlanta International Airport fills 1.92 million airline seats each week. That totals more than 99.8 billion seats per year! Approximately 967,050 planes depart and arrive at this airport every year. With parking lots, runways, maintenance facilities, and other buildings, the Hartsfield terminal complex covers about 130 acres (53 ha). Hartsfield-Jackson Atlanta International Airport has a north and a south terminal, an underground train, and six concourses with a total of 154 domestic and 28 international gates.

busiest airports

seats per week, in millions

Airport	Seats
Hartsfield-Jackson Atlanta Intl., USA	1.92
Beijing Capital Intl., China	1.91
Tokyo Haneda Intl., Japan	1.81
London Heathrow, UK	1.66
Dubai Intl., UAE	1.58

T E R M I N A L   N O R T H

✈ Gates T9-T15	South Ticketing/Check-In	All Gates ✈
↑	South Baggage Claim	→
P North Parking	South Parking P	Gates T1-T8 ✈ →
		Restrooms

country that produces the most cars

China

China leads the world in car production by creating 14.1 million vehicles annually. Approximately 44 percent of all the cars produced in the country are Chinese brands, including Lifan, Geely, Chery, and several others. International brands with factories in China include Volkswagen, General Motors, and Honda. Most of the cars that are produced in China are also sold there. Fewer than 400,000 cars are exported each year. China's growth in the car production industry is fairly recent. Since the country joined the World Trade Organization in 2001, China's car production has grown by about 1 million vehicles annually.

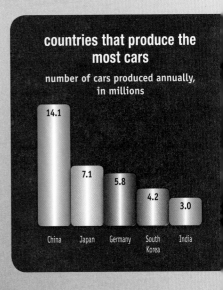

countries that produce the most cars

number of cars produced annually, in millions

China	Japan	Germany	South Korea	India
14.1	7.1	5.8	4.2	3.0

greenest city

Reykjavík

The Icelandic city of Reykjavík was ranked the greenest city in the world by *GlobalPost* because of its commitment to reducing its carbon footprint and its pledge to improve the environment. Reykjavík runs almost entirely on geothermal power and hydroelectricity. In its quest to become the most environmentally responsible city in Europe, Reykjavík uses only hydrogen-powered buses. The city's university now integrates environmental issues and sustainability into most classes. Reykjavík is made up of about 170,000 people, which is about 60 percent of the country's population.

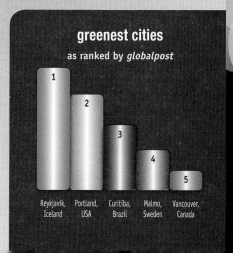

greenest cities

as ranked by *globalpost*

1	2	3	4	5
Reykjavik, Iceland	Portland, USA	Curitiba, Brazil	Malmo, Sweden	Vancouver, Canada

Money Records

Lunch Money

Fast-food fans fork over different amounts of cash, depending upon where they live. People living in Juneau, Alaska, for instance, pay $4.82 for a McDonald's quarter-pounder, while folks in Conway, Arkansas, pay just $2.24. In addition to cost of living, this is also due to shipping the food to remote places.

Does It Include Lessons?

A Fender Stratocaster became the most expensive guitar in history when it sold for $2.7 million in 2005. The guitar was autographed by 20 music legends, including Mick Jagger, Keith Richards, Eric Clapton, Jimmy Page, Pete Townsend, Paul McCartney, and Bryan Adams. It was auctioned off at the Reach Out to Asia benefit to raise money for the victims of the 2004 tsunami.

Hold the Anchovies

The Louis XIII pizza costs $12,000 a pie! Instead of pepperoni, the culinary masterpiece is topped with lobster, caviar, eight different types of cheese, and hand-picked Australian river salt. For this price, Chef Renato Viola will send his chefs anywhere in Italy to prepare one for a customer.

How Could She Say No?

When rapper Jay-Z proposed to Beyoncé, he pulled out a $5 million diamond ring—the most expensive celebrity ring on record. The flawless, 18-carat emerald-cut diamond is set in platinum. The couple secretly tied the knot in April 2008, and Beyoncé first flashed her rock in September of that year at the Fashion Rock benefit in New York.

Stinking Rich for $200, Alex

With more than $3.45 million, Brad Rutter of Pennsylvania is the biggest winner on *Jeopardy!* since the television game show began in 1984. His total winnings are a combination of his regular and tournament appearances. Next in line is Ken Jennings, who won $2.5 million and set a record for the most consecutive wins with 74.

Books for Bucks

At $228,000, a first edition of *Harry Potter and the Philosopher's Stone*—a rare 1997 copy with author J.K. Rowling's notes in the margins—was the top seller at a fundraiser in May 2013. The proceeds from the auction benefitted the English Pen—an association founded to promote literature and free speech. The US edition of the book was titled *Harry Potter and the Sorcerer's Stone*.

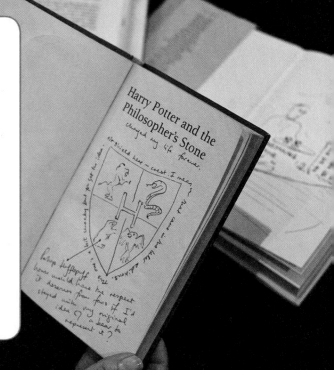

Picture-Perfect Price

In May 2013, German artist Gerhard Richter sold a giant oil painting for $37 million at Sotheby's. This is the highest price ever fetched for a work by a living artist. The 9-foot-by-9-foot (0.9 m by 0.9 m) painting, titled *Domplatz, Mailand,* is of Milan's Cathedral Square and was completed in 1968.

most expensive hotel suites

Royal Penthouse Suite

Guests better bring their wallets to the President Wilson Hotel in Geneva, Switzerland—the Royal Penthouse Suite costs $65,000 a night! That means a weeklong stay would total $455,000, which is almost twice the price of buying the average house in the US. The suite is reserved for heads of state and celebrities, and offers beautiful views of the Alps and Lake Geneva. The 18,082-square-foot (1,680 sq m) four-bedroom luxury suite has a private elevator and marble bathrooms. The state-of-the-art security system includes bulletproof doors and windows.

most expensive hotel suites
price per night, in US dollars

65,000	45,000	41,800	37,500	35,500
Royal Penthouse Suite, President Wilson Hotel, Switzerland	Presidential Suite, Raj Palace, India	Ty Warner Penthouse, Four Seasons, USA	Penthouse Suite, Hotel Martinez, France	Hugh Hefner Sky Villa, Palms Casino & Resort, USA

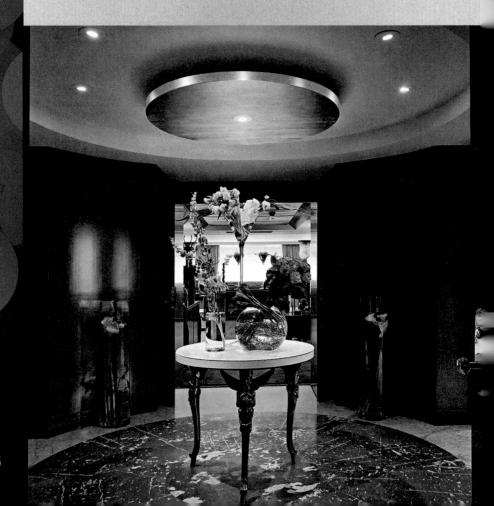

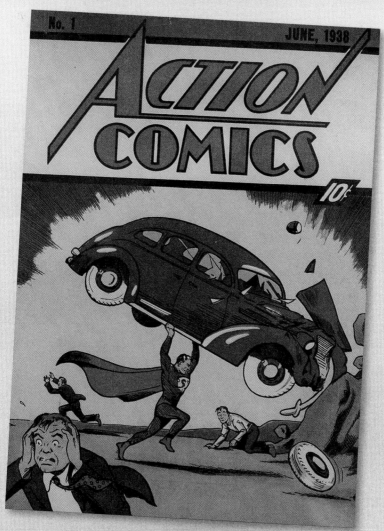

most expensive comic book

Action Comics, No. 1

Action Comics, No. 1 sold for $2.1 million at auction in November 2011. This comic was published in April 1938 and introduced Superman to the world. Known as the world's first superhero comic, it featured the Man of Steel lifting up a car on its cover. It originally sold for 10 cents. Comic artists Jerry Siegel and Joe Shuster created the book and were paid $10 per page. About 200,000 copies were printed, but only about 100 survive today. Another copy of the same issue was auctioned off in March 2010, but fetched only $1.5 million because it was not in as good condition.

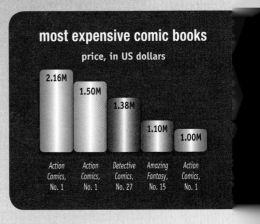

most expensive comic books

price, in US dollars

2.16M	1.50M	1.38M	1.10M	1.00M
Action Comics, No. 1	Action Comics, No. 1	Detective Comics, No. 27	Amazing Fantasy, No. 15	Action Comics, No. 1

most expensive tv series ad slot in 2012

Sunday Night Football

For every 30-second commercial shown during *Sunday Night Football* in 2012, advertisers had to pay a whopping $545,142. That breaks down to more than $18,171 per second! That's also the same cost as 218 Super Bowl XLVII tickets. *Sunday Night Football*—which was also the highest-rated show in 2012—is seen by about 21 million people each week, and advertisers want to capture their attention. And even though that seems high, when advertisers measure it by the cost per thousand viewers, it comes out to just $25.

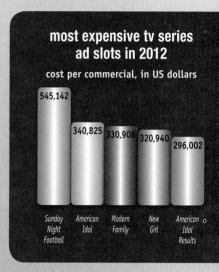

most expensive tv series ad slots in 2012

cost per commercial, in US dollars

Sunday Night Football	American Idol	Modern Family	New Girl	American Idol Results
545,142	340,825	330,908	320,940	296,002

Cris Collinsworth and Al Michaels of *Sunday Night Football*

most valuable production car

Lamborghini Veneno

The Lamborghini Veneno costs a whopping $3.9 million—about 74 times the average median income in the United States! The super sportscar boasts a 750-horsepower, V-12 engine and a 7-speed manual transmission. The Veneno can reach a top speed of 220 miles per hour (354 km/hr). It can accelerate from 0 to 60 in about 2.8 seconds. The car was created to celebrate Lamborghini's 50th anniversary. Only three Venenos will be produced, and each will be metallic gray. The car was named after a famous Spanish fighting bull from the 1900s.

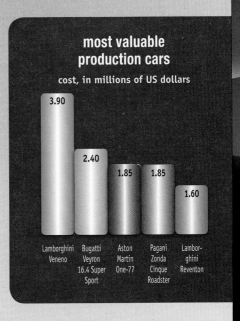

most valuable production cars

cost, in millions of US dollars

Lamborghini Veneno	Bugatti Veyron 16.4 Super Sport	Aston Martin One-77	Pagani Zonda Cinque Roadster	Lamborghini Reventon
3.90	2.40	1.85	1.85	1.60

most expensive sports memorabilia

Babe Ruth Jersey

In April 2012, a Babe Ruth jersey sold for more than $4.4 million during a Lelands.com auction, making it the most expensive piece of sports memorabilia ever. The New York Yankees jersey is one of the earliest Ruth ever wore, dating back to the 1920s. The jersey was in high demand, with 36 different people bidding on it. The winning bidder chose to remain anonymous. Before the jersey went up for auction, it was on display for five years at a Baltimore museum. Other Ruth items were also sold during the auction, including a 1930s hat for $537,000, and a bat that sold for $591,000.

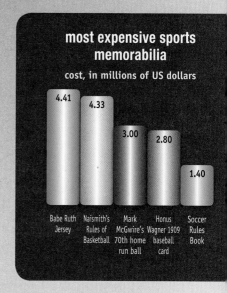

most expensive sports memorabilia

cost, in millions of US dollars

Babe Ruth Jersey	Naismith's Rules of Basketball	Mark McGwire's 70th home run ball	Honus Wagner 1909 baseball card	Soccer Rules Book
4.41	4.33	3.00	2.80	1.40

most valuable sports brand

Nike

The Nike brand is worth more than $15.9 billion worldwide. Nike leads the footwear industry with 38 percent of the market. In 2012, Nike signed a deal to become the official licensed-apparel maker of the NFL for the next five years. During 2012, Nike earned more than $24.1 billion. The company was founded in 1972 by Bill Bowerman and Phil Knight, and it has grown to include many successful subsidiaries such as Converse, Umbro, and Cole Haan. Nike operates in 160 countries across six continents, and employs 35,000 people.

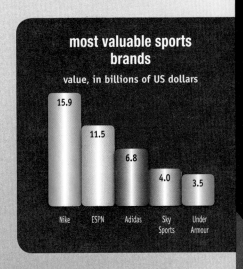

most valuable sports brands

value, in billions of US dollars

Brand	Value
Nike	15.9
ESPN	11.5
Adidas	6.8
Sky Sports	4.0
Under Armour	3.5

most valuable football team

Dallas Cowboys

Worth $2.1 billion, the Dallas Cowboys are the most valuable team in the National Football League for the sixth year in a row. In addition to ticket sales, the Cowboys have several side businesses that bring in the cash. In 2008, they launched Legends Hospitality Management, a company that consults with other team owners to maximize earnings. They also started Silver Star Merchandising to make and distribute team apparel. Cowboys Stadium has 320 suites and 15,000 club seats, and generates $500 million in revenue annually. The team and its loyal fans have enjoyed 21 division championships, 10 conference championships, and 5 Super Bowl championships since the franchise began in 1960.

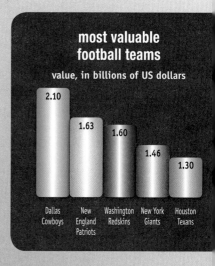

most valuable football teams

value, in billions of US dollars

Dallas Cowboys	New England Patriots	Washington Redskins	New York Giants	Houston Texans
2.10	1.63	1.60	1.46	1.30

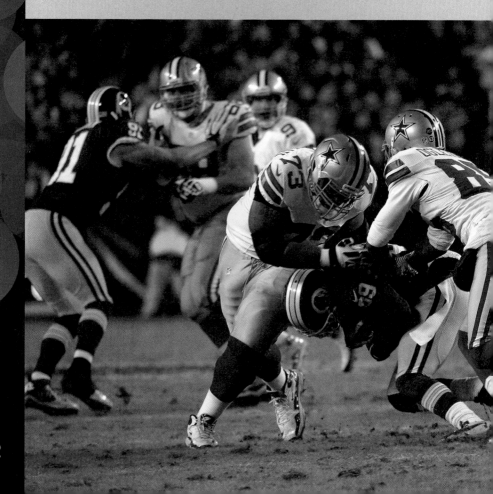

most valuable hockey team

Toronto Maple Leafs

The Toronto Maple Leafs are worth $1 billion, which is $281 million more than the average pro hockey team's value. The team's top ranking is largely due to strong ticket sales and lucrative television deals. Although Toronto won 13 Stanley Cups between 1917 and 1967, they have not won a cup in 46 years, which is the longest losing streak in the league. Toronto was one of the six teams that formed the National Hockey League in 1917. Their home arena is called Air Canada Centre.

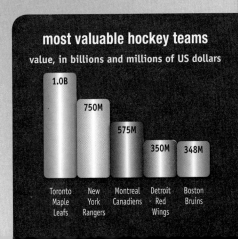

most valuable hockey teams

value, in billions and millions of US dollars

Toronto Maple Leafs	New York Rangers	Montreal Canadiens	Detroit Red Wings	Boston Bruins
1.0B	750M	575M	350M	348M

most valuable soccer team

Manchester United

Manchester United Red Devils top the soccer charts with an overall value in 2012 of $2.23 billion—an increase of 20 percent from 2011. The team, which brought in $532 million in revenue in 2012, was founded in 1878. Since then, they have won 19 domestic league championships, and they hold the record for the most Football Association Challenge Cup victories with 11 wins. Manchester United has also won three European Cups and one UEFA Cup. Captain Nemanja Vidic has led the team since 2011, and several players have more than 300 games played, including Wayne Rooney, Patrice Evra, and Michael Carrick.

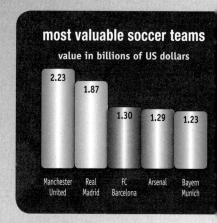

most valuable soccer teams

value in billions of US dollars

Manchester United	Real Madrid	FC Barcelona	Arsenal	Bayern Munich
2.23	1.87	1.30	1.29	1.23

most expensive sports team purchase

Los Angeles Dodgers

In 2012, Magic Johnson and the Guggenheim Partners bought the Los Angeles Dodgers for $2 billion. That's four times higher than what the team sold for in 2004. Baseball executive Stan Kasten became the team's president, and Johnson oversees recruiting free agents. The team was established in Brooklyn, NY, in 1883, and later moved to Los Angeles in 1958. The Dodgers have won 21 National League pennants and 6 World Series titles. The team plays at Dodger Stadium, which is the third-oldest ballpark in Major League Baseball.

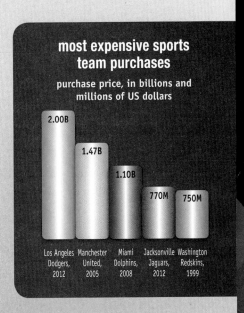

most expensive sports team purchases

purchase price, in billions and millions of US dollars

- 2.00B — Los Angeles Dodgers, 2012
- 1.47B — Manchester United, 2005
- 1.10B — Miami Dolphins, 2008
- 770M — Jacksonville Jaguars, 2012
- 750M — Washington Redskins, 1999

united states' bestselling automobiles

Ford F-Series

Ford sold 645,316 F-Series trucks during 2012. The F-Series originated in 1948, when the F-1 (half ton), the F-2 (three-quarter ton), and the F-3 (Heavy Duty) were introduced. Since then, many modifications and new editions have been introduced, including the F-150. The modern F-150 sports a V-8 engine and the option of a regular, extended, or crew cab. The bed size ranges from 5.5 feet (1.6 m) to 8 feet (2.4 km). The Platinum F-150—the top-of-the-line version—features platinum chrome wheels, a fancy grille design, leather upholstery, and heated seats.

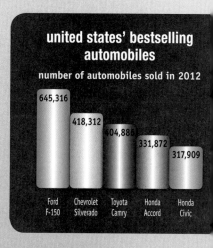

united states' bestselling automobiles

number of automobiles sold in 2012

Ford F-150	Chevrolet Silverado	Toyota Camry	Honda Accord	Honda Civic
645,316	418,312	404,886	331,872	317,909

largest global retailer

Walmart

Megadiscount retail chain Walmart had more than $446 billion in sales during 2012. Walmart serves more than 200 million customers each week at its more than 9,600 stores. Located in 28 countries, the company employs more than 1.4 million people in the United States and another 700,000 worldwide. This makes Walmart one of the largest private employers in North America. Walmart also believes in giving back to the community, and donated more than $1 billion in cash and contributions to charities around the world in 2012. Walmart is currently ranked number one in the *Fortune 500* list of most profitable companies.

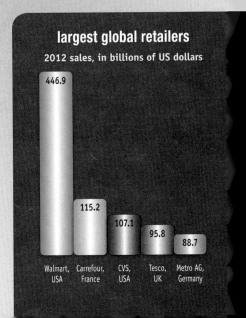

largest global retailers
2012 sales, in billions of US dollars

Walmart, USA	446.9
Carrefour, France	115.2
CVS, USA	107.1
Tesco, UK	95.8
Metro AG, Germany	88.7

largest global food franchise

Subway

There are 35,920 Subway restaurants located throughout the world. There are 24,722 franchises in the United States, and another 11,198 international locations. Subway, which is owned by Doctor's Associates, Inc., had global sales totaling $16.6 billion in 2012—up about 10 percent from the previous year. The sandwich company was started by Fred DeLuca in 1965, and began franchising in 1974. Start-up fees run between $84,000 and $258,000, and 100 percent of the company is franchised. About 65 percent of franchises own more than one location.

largest global food franchises

number of franchises

Subway	McDonald's	KFC	Pizza Hut	Burger King
35,920	33,510	17,401	13,747	12,512

largest retail franchise

7-Eleven

There are 43,912 7-Eleven convenience stores located around the world. Approximately 96 percent of these stores are franchised, with 6,497 locations in the United States and 37,415 locations internationally. 7-Eleven earned $76.6 billion in sales in 2012. The store chain is ranked number two on the *Forbes* Top 20 Franchises for the Buck list, meaning that investors have a very good chance of making a profit on their stores. The stores sell about 275 baked goods every minute, more than 2,300 fresh sandwiches each hour, and 13 million Slurpee beverages each month. Approximately 25 percent of Americans live within a mile (1.6 km) of a 7-Eleven store.

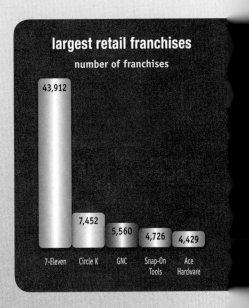

largest retail franchises
number of franchises

7-Eleven	Circle K	GNC	Snap-On Tools	Ace Hardware
43,912	7,452	5,560	4,726	4,429

Pop Culture Records

books
television
movies
music
theater

Always a Winner

In 2012, Julia Louis-Dreyfus became only the second person ever to win an Emmy as a regular cast member of three different series—*Seinfeld* (1996), *The New Adventures of Old Christine* (2006), and *Veep* (2012). Actress Tyne Daly also accomplished this in 2003.

Wreck-It Walt?

Disney's Wreck-It Ralph features some coded references to the company's founder. A billboard outside the film's Litwak's Family Fun Center advertises, "Double U Dee's"—which sounds like W.D.'s, Walt Disney's initials. Also, the high score of Wreck-It Ralph's game cabinet is 120,501. When broken out into a date—12-05-01—it becomes Walt Disney's birthday.

Timing Is Everything

Adele's "Skyfall"—the title song for the latest James Bond movie of the same name—was released at 0:07 a.m. on October 5, 2012. It's the first Bond theme song to ever debut in the top ten of the US Billboard Hot 100.

PSY-co Fans

Gangnam Style became the most-watched YouTube video ever in 2012 with more than 1 billion views since it was released in February 2010. At its peak, the video was viewed about 4,000 times a minute. *Gangnam Style* also holds the record for the most likes on YouTube with more than 2 million.

Look Out Below

The 2012 blockbuster *Marvel's The Avengers* had a spectacular chase scene involving Loki (Tom Hiddleston), Hawkeye (Jeremy Renner), and Agent Maria Hill (Cobie Smulders). This was actually filmed in Pennsylvania, about 300 feet (91 m) belowground in what used to be the world's largest mushroom-growing facility. It took months to prep the 150 miles (241.4 km) of tunnels for the shoot because the structure had no power or electricity.

More D'Oh!

With more than 500 episodes, *The Simpsons* is the longest-running animated sitcom. The show—which is currently in its 25th season—is seen by about 150 million people worldwide each week. It takes about six months and 480 animators to create just one half-hour episode!

Wicked Good

The set of Broadway's *Wicked* is quite elaborate—the scenery weighs about 175,000 pounds (79,378 kg) and uses 5 miles (8 km) of cable to animate it. The dragon's wingspan measures the same length as a Cessna 172 plane. And to set the scene with mysterious fog, the show uses about 250 pounds (113.3 kg) of dry ice each performance.

highest-paid author of books for young people

Jeff Kinney

Thanks to his bestselling Diary of a Wimpy Kid series, author Jeff Kinney raked in $25 million in 2012. His latest book, *The Third Wheel*, was released in November 2012 with a 6.8-million-copy print run. Greg Heffley, the star of Kinney's series, endures the hardships of middle school with hilarious ups and downs. Although Kinney came up with the idea for the series in 1998, his first book was not published until 2007. Kinney's stories and comics were first published in daily installments on funbrain.com in 2006. Three of the books have also been made into successful movies.

highest-paid authors of books for young people

income in 2012, in millions of US dollars

Jeff Kinney	Suzanne Collins	J.K. Rowling	Stephenie Meyer	Rick Riordan
25	20	17	14	13

highest-paid tv actors

Ashton Kutcher

Ashton Kutcher pulled in $24 million in 2012 for his role as Walden Schmidt—a brokenhearted millionaire—on *Two and a Half Men*. Kutcher debuted on the hit CBS comedy in September 2011 to replace Charlie Sheen. More than 27.7 million people tuned in to see his first episode—the largest audience in the show's history. Before joining *Two and a Half Men*, Kutcher starred in Fox's *That '70s Show*, and several movies, including *Dude, Where's My Car?*, *The Butterfly Effect*, and *What Happens in Vegas*. He also produced a reality show, *Punk'd*, for MTV.

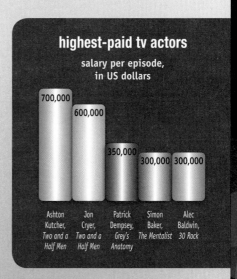

highest-paid tv actors
salary per episode, in US dollars

Ashton Kutcher, *Two and a Half Men*	Jon Cryer, *Two and a Half Men*	Patrick Dempsey, *Grey's Anatomy*	Simon Baker, *The Mentalist*	Alec Baldwin, *30 Rock*
700,000	600,000	350,000	300,000	300,000

highest-paid tv actress

Mariska Hargitay

Law & Order: Special Victims Unit actress Mariska Hargitay earns $385,000 per episode for her role as Detective Olivia Benson. Since the NBC crime drama—also known simply as *SVU*—began in 1999, Hargitay has won an Emmy and a Golden Globe for her performance. The series focuses on the 16th Precinct of the New York Police Department, and follows the detectives and lawyers from when the crime is committed to how it plays out in the courtroom. The show is a spinoff of the original *Law & Order* series, and was the second in the franchise. *SVU* draws about 6.3 million views each week.

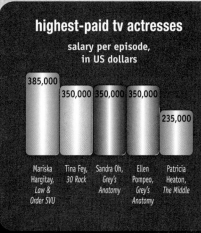

highest-paid tv actresses

salary per episode, in US dollars

385,000	350,000	350,000	350,000	235,000
Mariska Hargitay, *Law & Order SVU*	Tina Fey, *30 Rock*	Sandra Oh, *Grey's Anatomy*	Ellen Pompeo, *Grey's Anatomy*	Patricia Heaton, *The Middle*

tv show with the most emmy awards

Frasier

Frasier—a hugely popular show that ran between 1993 and 2004—picked up 37 Emmy Awards during its 11 seasons. The sitcom focused on the life and family of psychiatrist Dr. Frasier Crane, played by Kelsey Grammer. His costars included David Hyde Pierce, John Mahoney, Peri Gilpin, and Jane Leeves. Some of the 37 awards the series won include Outstanding Comedy Series, Lead Actor in a Comedy Series, Supporting Actor in a Comedy Series, Directing in a Comedy Series, Editing, and Art Direction.

tv shows with the most emmy awards

emmys won

Frasier	Saturday Night Live	The Mary Tyler Moore Show	Cheers	Hill Street Blues
37	36	29	28	26

77

tv show with the most consecutive emmy awards

The Daily Show with Jon Stewart

The Daily Show with Jon Stewart has won an Emmy Award for Outstanding Variety, Music or Comedy series for ten consecutive seasons between 2003 and 2012. In total, the show has received 27 Emmy nominations, and has won 18 of them. Although it is considered a fake news show, the program often uses actual recent news stories and delivers them with a funny or sarcastic spin. The show began in 1996, and it is the longest-running program on Comedy Central. *The Daily Show* was hosted by Craig Kilborn until 1998, when Kilborn was replaced by Stewart.

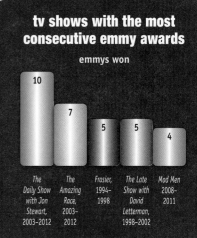

tv shows with the most consecutive emmy awards

emmys won

The Daily Show with Jon Stewart, 2003–2012	The Amazing Race, 2003–2012	Frasier, 1994–1998	The Late Show with David Letterman, 1998–2002	Mad Men 2008–2011
10	7	5	5	4

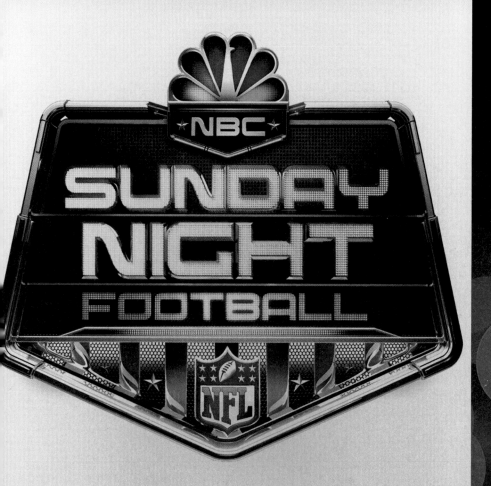

most popular tv show

NBC Sunday Night Football

An average of 21.2 million fans tuned in each week to watch *NBC Sunday Night Football* in 2012. The show, which kicked off on September 5th and ended on December 30, is currently in its eighth year. Commentators Al Michaels, Cris Collinsworth, and Michele Tafoya announce the play-by-play, while studio hosts Bob Costas, Dan Patrick, Tony Dungy, Rodney Harrison, and Hines Ward break down the game during the half-time and post-game shows.

most popular tv shows
viewers per week, in millions

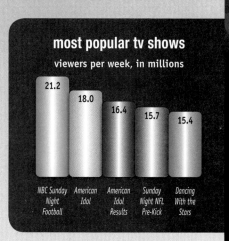

NBC Sunday Night Football	American Idol	American Idol Results	Sunday Night NFL Pre-Kick	Dancing With the Stars
21.2	18.0	16.4	15.7	15.4

Adam Sandler

celebrities with the most kids' choice awards

Adam Sandler & Will Smith

Kids love funny actors! With their votes, Adam Sandler and Will Smith have each won 9 Nickelodeon Kids' Choice Awards since the show began in 1988. Sandler's awards include Favorite Movie Actor (1999, 2000, 2003, 2005, 2007, 2012), Favorite Voice From an Animated Movie (2003, 2013), and a Wannabe Award (2004). Smith's awards include Favorite TV Actor (1991), Favorite Movie Actor (1998, 2006, 2009), Favorite Male Singer (1999, 2000), Wannabe Award (2003), Favorite Voice From an Animated Movie (2005), and a Hall of Fame entry (1997).

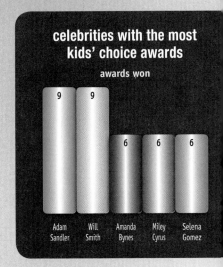

celebrities with the most kids' choice awards

awards won

Adam Sandler	Will Smith	Amanda Bynes	Miley Cyrus	Selena Gomez
9	9	6	6	6

highest-paid director/producer

Michael Bay

Michael Bay earned $160 million in 2012, which is about 5,731 times what the average US worker earns. One of the biggest sources of income was *Transformers: Dark of the Moon*—the third installment of the Transformers franchise—which earned more than $352 million. Some of Bay's previous successes include *Armageddon*, *Pearl Harbor*, and *Bad Boys*. Before Bay worked on movies, he directed commercials and created music videos for artists including Aerosmith and Tina Turner.

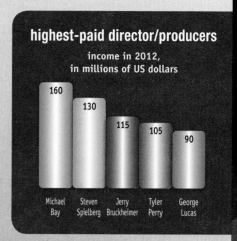

highest-paid director/producers

income in 2012, in millions of US dollars

Michael Bay	Steven Spielberg	Jerry Bruckheimer	Tyler Perry	George Lucas
160	130	115	105	90

highest-paid celebrity couple

Jay-Z & Beyoncé

Powerhouse performers Jay-Z and Beyoncé earned $78 million in 2012. Beyoncé, whose contribution to the family income was $40 million, released her fourth studio album, 4, in June 2011. The album sold more than 300,000 copies in one week and became the singer's fourth number one album. Beyoncé also has several side ventures that bring in extra cash, including an endorsement deal with Pepsi and her own line of perfume. Jay-Z contributed $38 million, mainly from album sales and tour proceeds from *Watch the Throne*—a collaboration with fellow hip-hop star Kanye West.

highest-paid celebrity couples

combined income in 2012, in millions of US dollars

Jay-Z & Beyoncé	Tom Brady & Gisele Bundchen	David Beckham & Victoria Beckham	Brad Pitt & Angelina Jolie	Will Smith & Jada Pinkett Smith
78	72	54	45	40

Ben-Hur, Titanic & The Lord of the Rings: The Return of the King

The only three films in Hollywood history to win 11 Academy Awards are *Ben-Hur*, *Titanic*, and *The Lord of the Rings: The Return of the King*. Some of the Oscar wins for *Ben-Hur*—a biblical epic based on an 1880 novel by General Lew Wallace—include Best Actor (Charlton Heston) and Director (William Wyler). Some of *Titanic*'s Oscars include Best Cinematography, Visual Effects, and Costume Design. *The Lord of the Rings: The Return of the King* is the final film in the epic trilogy based on the works of J. R. R. Tolkien. With 11 awards, it is the most successful movie in Academy Awards history because it won every category in which it was nominated. Some of these wins include Best Picture, Director (Peter Jackson), and Costume Design.

movies with the most oscars

oscars won

Ben-Hur, 1959	Titanic, 1997	The Lord of the Rings: The Return of the King, 2004	West Side Story, 1961	The Last Emperor, 1987
11	11	11	10	9

Presenters and the cast of *The Lord of the Rings* (Peter Jackson in front)

actress with the most oscar nominations

Meryl Streep

Meryl Streep is the most nominated actress in the history of the Academy Awards with 17 chances to win a statue. Her first nomination came in 1979 for *The Deer Hunter*, and was followed by *Kramer vs. Kramer* (1980), *The French Lieutenant's Woman* (1981), *Sophie's Choice* (1982), *Silkwood* (1983), *Out of Africa* (1985), *Ironweed* (1987), *A Cry in the Dark* (1988), *Postcards From the Edge* (1990), *The Bridges of Madison County* (1995), *One True Thing* (1998), *Music of the Heart* (1999), *Adaptation* (2002), *The Devil Wears Prada* (2006), *Doubt* (2008), *Julie and Julia* (2009), and *The Iron Lady* (2012). Streep won her first Academy Award for *Kramer vs. Kramer*, her second for *Sophie's Choice*, and a third for *The Iron Lady*.

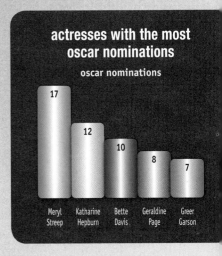

actresses with the most oscar nominations

oscar nominations

Meryl Streep	Katharine Hepburn	Bette Davis	Geraldine Page	Greer Garson
17	12	10	8	7

actor with the most oscar nominations

Jack Nicholson

Jack Nicholson has been nominated for a record 12 Oscars during his distinguished career. He is one of only three men to have been nominated for an acting Academy Award at least once every decade for five decades. He was nominated for eight Best Actor awards for his roles in *Five Easy Pieces* (1970), *The Last Detail* (1973), *Chinatown* (1974), *One Flew Over the Cuckoo's Nest* (1975), *Prizzi's Honor* (1985), *Ironweed* (1987), *As Good as It Gets* (1997), and *About Schmidt* (2002). He was nominated for Best Supporting Actor for *Easy Rider* (1969), *Reds* (1981), *Terms of Endearment* (1983), and *A Few Good Men* (1992). Nicholson picked up statues for *One Flew Over the Cuckoo's Nest*, *Terms of Endearment*, and *As Good as It Gets*.

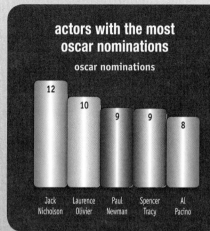

actors with the most oscar nominations

oscar nominations

Jack Nicholson	Laurence Olivier	Paul Newman	Spencer Tracy	Al Pacino
12	10	9	9	8

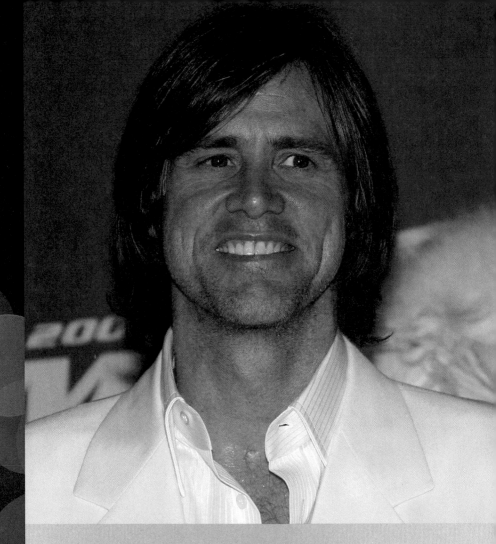

actor with the most mtv movie awards

Jim Carrey

Jim Carrey has won 11 MTV Movie Awards since the television station began awarding them in 1992. He has won the award for Best Comedic Performance five times, for his roles in *Dumb & Dumber* (1995), *Ace Ventura II: When Nature Calls* (1996), *The Cable Guy* (1997), *Liar Liar* (1998), and *Yes Man* (2009). Carrey won the award for Best Male Performance twice, for *Ace Ventura II: When Nature Calls* and *The Truman Show* (1999). He also won awards for Best Kiss for *Dumb & Dumber*, Best Villain for *The Cable Guy*, and the MTV Generation Award in 2006.

actors with the most mtv movie awards
awards won

Jim Carrey	Robert Pattinson	Mike Myers	Adam Sandler	Johnny Depp
11	10	7	6	5

actress with the most mtv movie awards

Kristen Stewart

Kristen Stewart, who rose to fame playing Bella Swan in the Twilight saga, won seven MTV Movie Awards for her role. She picked up her first two awards—Best Female Performance and Best Kiss—in 2009 for *Twilight*. She shared the Best Kiss award with co-star Robert Pattinson. A year later, she picked up the same two awards for *New Moon*. In 2011, Stewart nabbed the same two again for *Eclipse*. Stewart's most recent award win came in 2012, when she once again shared the Best Kiss award with Robert Pattinson for the 2011 Twilight film, *Breaking Dawn: Part One*.

actresses with the most mtv movie awards

awards won

Kristen Stewart	Alicia Silverstone	Uma Thurman	Sandra Bullock	Drew Barrymore
7	4	4	4	3

Rosie Huntington-Whiteley

Rosie Huntington-Whiteley has only been in one movie, but it was a successful one! *Transformers: Dark of the Moon,* which was released in 2011, made more than $352 million at the box office. Huntington-Whiteley played Carly Spencer in the third installment of the Transformers series, and starred opposite Shia LeBeouf. She was nominated for a Teen Choice Award, and won a CinemaCon Award Female Star of Tomorrow Award for her performance. In addition to acting, Huntington-Whiteley is also a well-known model for Prada, Burberry, and Victoria's Secret.

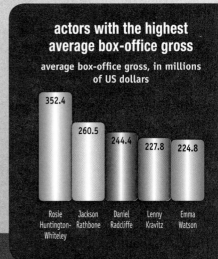

actors with the highest average box-office gross

average box-office gross, in millions of US dollars

Rosie Huntington-Whiteley	Jackson Rathbone	Daniel Radcliffe	Lenny Kravitz	Emma Watson
352.4	260.5	244.4	227.8	224.8

actor with the highest career box-office gross

Frank Welker

Frank Welker's movies have a combined total gross of $6.45 billion. Although movie fans might not recognize Welker's name or face, they would probably recognize many of his voices. Welker is a voice actor, and has worked on more than 90 movies in the last 25 years. Some of his most famous voices include Megatron, Curious George, and Scooby-Doo. Welker's most profitable movies include *How the Grinch Stole Christmas*, *Godzilla*, and *101 Dalmatians*.

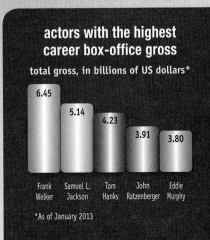

actors with the highest career box-office gross

total gross, in billions of US dollars*

Frank Welker	Samuel L. Jackson	Tom Hanks	John Ratzenberger	Eddie Murphy
6.45	5.14	4.23	3.91	3.80

*As of January 2013

top-grossing animated movie

Toy Story 3

With earnings of more than $1.06 billion worldwide, *Toy Story 3* has easily become the highest-grossing animated movie in history. It is also the seventh-highest-grossing movie ever. The Disney-Pixar movie opened on June 18, 2010, and earned $110 million during its first three days in theaters. The plot of the third installment of the Toy Story franchise follows Woody as he leads the other toys out of a day-care center where they were mistakenly delivered. The toys' famous voices included Tom Hanks (Woody), Tim Allen (Buzz), Joan Cusack (Jessie), and John Ratzenberger (Hamm).

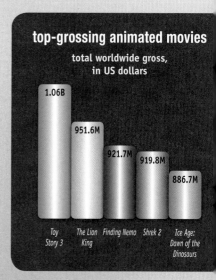

top-grossing animated movies
total worldwide gross, in US dollars

1.06B	951.6M	921.7M	919.8M	886.7M
Toy Story 3	The Lion King	Finding Nemo	Shrek 2	Ice Age: Dawn of the Dinosaurs

movie with the most successful domestic opening weekend

Marvel's The Avengers

On May 4, 2012, people flocked to theaters and spent more than $207 million to see *Marvel's The Avengers*. The movie has a worldwide gross of $1.51 billion, and is the third-highest-grossing movie of all time. DVD sales added another $68 million. The movie tells the story of the comic book superheroes including Iron Man, Captain America, the Hulk, and Thor, and its stars include Robert Downey, Jr., Samuel L. Jackson, Mark Ruffalo, Scarlett Johansson, and Chris Hemsworth. It was directed by Joss Whedon and released by Walt Disney Studios. *Marvel's The Avengers* had a budget of about $220 million.

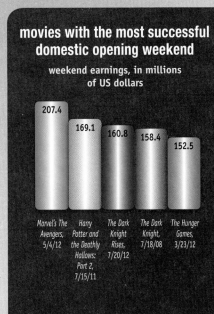

movies with the most successful domestic opening weekend

weekend earnings, in millions of US dollars

Marvel's The Avengers, 5/4/12	Harry Potter and the Deathly Hallows: Part 2, 7/15/11	The Dark Knight Rises, 7/20/12	The Dark Knight, 7/18/08	The Hunger Games, 3/23/12
207.4	169.1	160.8	158.4	152.5

top-grossing movie

Avatar

Avatar, James Cameron's science-fiction epic, was released in December 2009 and grossed more than $2.78 billion worldwide in less than two months. Starring Sigourney Weaver, Sam Worthington, and Zoe Saldana, *Avatar* cost more than $230 million to make. Cameron began working on the film in 1994, and it was eventually filmed in 3-D, with special cameras made just for the movie. Due to *Avatar*'s overwhelming success, Cameron is already planning two sequels.

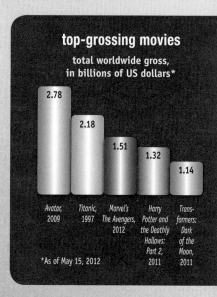

top-grossing movies
total worldwide gross, in billions of US dollars*

Avatar, 2009	Titanic, 1997	Marvel's The Avengers, 2012	Harry Potter and the Deathly Hallows: Part 2, 2011	Trans-formers: Dark of the Moon, 2011
2.78	2.18	1.51	1.32	1.14

*As of May 15, 2012

most successful movie franchise

Harry Potter

The eight movies in the Harry Potter franchise have collectively earned $7.70 billion. The series, which began in November 2001, is based on the bestselling books by J.K. Rowling. They chronicle the adventures of a young wizard—Harry Potter—as he grows up and learns of the great power he possesses. The highest-grossing movie in the franchise is the last one—*Harry Potter and the Deathly Hallows: Part 2*—which earned $1.3 billion worldwide. The leads of the movie, including Daniel Radcliffe, Rupert Grint, and Emma Watson, have become some of the highest-paid young stars in Hollywood.

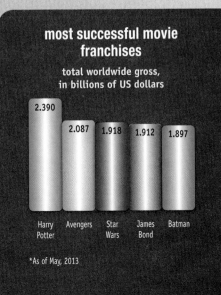

most successful movie franchises

total worldwide gross, in billions of US dollars

Harry Potter	Avengers	Star Wars	James Bond	Batman
2.390	2.087	1.918	1.912	1.897

*As of May, 2013

93

top-earning actor

Tom Cruise

Film legend Tom Cruise made $75 million in 2012, mostly due to his latest movie success—*Mission: Impossible–Ghost Protocol*. The fourth installment in the Mission Impossible franchise was the most profitable one and had a worldwide gross of $694 million. In addition to playing the lead character, Ethan Hunt, he also co-produced the movie. Cruise has starred in more than 30 movies, and his career box office total is $3.5 billion, with an average gross of $99 million per movie. Some of Cruise's other blockbusters include *War of the Worlds, The Last Samurai,* and *Minority Report.*

top-earning actors

2012 earnings, in millions of US dollars

Tom Cruise	Leonardo DiCaprio	Adam Sandler	Ben Stiller	Will Smith
75	37	37	33	30

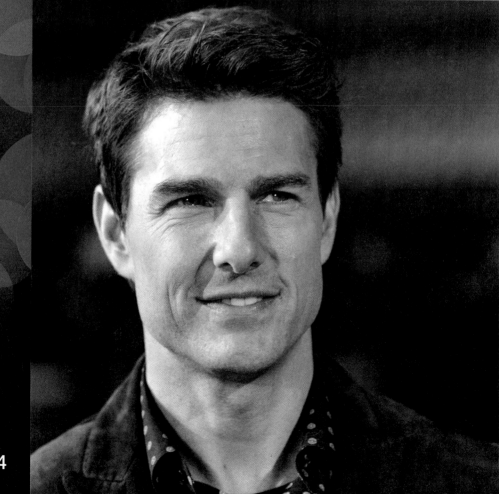

top-earning actress

Kristen Stewart

After starring in two huge movies that were released in 2012, Kristen Stewart tops the best-paid actress list with $34.5 million. Stewart reprised her role as Bella Swan for *The Twilight Saga: Breaking Dawn–Part 2*. The final installment in the film franchise earned $791 million worldwide. Stewart also played the title role in *Snow White and the Huntsman*, which earned more than $400 million globally. Since her first big role in 2002, Stewart's movies have earned more than $182 billion at the box office worldwide.

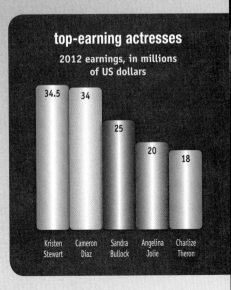

top-earning actresses

2012 earnings, in millions of US dollars

Kristen Stewart	Cameron Diaz	Sandra Bullock	Angelina Jolie	Charlize Theron
34.5	34	25	20	18

highest animated-movie budget

Tangled

Walt Disney Animation Studios budgeted $260 million for its fairy-tale remake, *Tangled*—and the big bucks paid off. *Tangled* more than doubled that figure with a worldwide gross of $586 million. Animators used computer-generated imagery (CGI) to create the film, but that was also combined with hand-drawn images to resemble classic fairy-tale films. Released in 2010, *Tangled* follows the journey of Rapunzel, from her tower deep in the forest to a reunion with her long-lost family. Mandy Moore, Zachary Levi, and Donna Murphy lent their voices to the main characters.

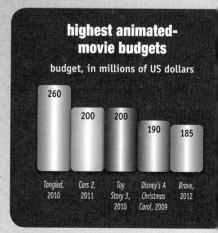

highest animated-movie budgets

budget, in millions of US dollars

Tangled, 2010	Cars 2, 2011	Toy Story 3, 2010	Disney's A Christmas Carol, 2009	Brave, 2012
260	200	200	190	185

highest movie budget

Pirates of the Caribbean: At World's End

With a budget of $300 million, the creators of *Pirates of the Caribbean: At World's End* spent the most money in movie history. And all of that money seems to have paid off. The third installment of the *Pirates* series opened in May 2007 and has since earned more than $963 million worldwide. It is among the top 20 highest-grossing films of all time. The Jerry Bruckheimer blockbuster starred Johnny Depp as Captain Jack Sparrow, Orlando Bloom as Will Turner, and Keira Knightley as Elizabeth Swann.

highest movie budgets

budget, in millions of US dollars

300	270	260	250	250
Pirates of the Caribbean: At World's End, 2007	Superman Returns, 2006	Tangled, 2010	The Hobbit: An Unexpected Journey, 2012	Spider-Man 3, 2007

movie that earned the most in a single day

Harry Potter and the Deathly Hallows: Part 2

On July 15, 2011, fans rushed to theaters to see *Harry Potter and the Deathly Hallows: Part 2*, spending $91 million in a single day. It was released in 4,375 theaters and earned an average of $20,816 per location. The final film in the wizard franchise went on to earn $1.3 billion worldwide—making it the fourth-highest-grossing movie of all time. It also holds the film record for earning $150 million in the shortest amount of time. *Harry Potter and the Deathly Hallows: Part 2* was nominated for three Academy Awards in 2011—Art Direction, Visual Effects, and Makeup.

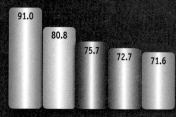

movies that earned the most in a single day

box-office earnings, in millions of US dollars

91.0	80.8	75.7	72.7	71.6
Harry Potter and the Deathly Hallows: Part 2, 7/15/11	Marvel's The Avengers, 5/4/12	The Dark Knight Rises, 7/20/12	The Twilight Saga: New Moon, 11/20/09	The Twilight Saga: Breaking Dawn– Part 1, 11/18/11

top-selling dvd

The Hunger Games

With more than 6 million copies sold, *The Hunger Games* was the top-selling DVD of 2012. Based on the bestselling novel by Suzanne Collins, the first movie in the four-film franchise debuted in theaters in March 2011 with opening-weekend box office receipts totaling $152 million. The movie stars Jennifer Lawrence as Katniss, Josh Hutcherson as Peeta, and Liam Hemsworth as Gale. The plot centers around Katniss, Peeta, and other young tributes who must engage in a battle to the death called the Hunger Games.

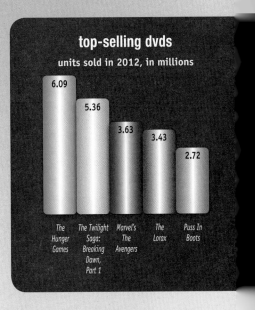

top-selling dvds
units sold in 2012, in millions

6.09	5.36	3.63	3.43	2.72
The Hunger Games	The Twilight Saga: Breaking Dawn, Part 1	Marvel's The Avengers	The Lorax	Puss In Boots

bestselling movie soundtrack

The Bodyguard

The soundtrack of *The Bodyguard* has sold more than 17 million copies since it was released in November 1992. The movie starred Kevin Costner as a former FBI agent in charge of a pop singer, played by Whitney Houston. Houston produced the soundtrack, along with Clive Davis, and it features three of Houston's biggest hits—"I Will Always Love You," "I Have Nothing," and "I'm Every Woman." The album picked up a Grammy for Album of the Year and reached number one on music charts worldwide, including Australia, Canada, France, Germany, and Japan.

bestselling movie soundtracks

units sold, in millions

The Bodyguard	Saturday Night Fever	Purple Rain	Forrest Gump	Titanic
17	15	13	12	11

united states' bestselling recording group

The Beatles

The Beatles have sold 177 million copies of their albums in the United States since their first official recording session in September 1962. In the two years that followed, they had 26 Top 40 singles. John Lennon, Paul McCartney, George Harrison, and Ringo Starr made up the "Fab Four," as the Beatles were known. Together they recorded many albums that are now considered rock masterpieces, such as *Rubber Soul*, *Sgt. Pepper's Lonely Hearts Club Band*, and *The Beatles*. The group broke up in 1969. In 2001, however, their newly released greatest hits album—*The Beatles 1*—reached the top of the charts. One of their best-known songs—"Yesterday"—is the most-recorded song in history, with about 2,500 different artists recording their own versions.

united states' bestselling recording groups

albums sold, in millions

177.0	111.5	100.0	74.5	71.0
The Beatles	Led Zeppelin	The Eagles	Pink Floyd	AC/DC

top-selling recording artist

Adele

English singer-songwriter Adele sold more than 5.1 million albums in 2012. She has released two albums—*19* and *21*—since her career began in 2006. The singer has picked up some prestigious awards during her short career. In 2008, she was nominated for four Grammys and won two—Best New Artist and Best Female Pop Vocal Performance. In 2011, she won six Grammys and became just the second woman in history to accomplish this in one evening (after Beyoncé in 2009). Some of Adele's wins included Song of the Year, Album of the Year, and Record of the Year.

top-selling recording artists

album sales in 2012, in millions

Adele	Taylor Swift	One Direction	Mumford and Son	Justin Bieber
5.16	4.06	2.97	2.14	1.89

most downloaded song

"Somebody That I Used to Know"

Singer-songwriter Goyte's huge breakthrough hit, "Somebody That I Used to Know" was downloaded more than 6.8 million times in 2012. The song is on the album *Making Mirrors*, which was Goyte's third independently released album. "Somebody That I Used to Know" reached the top spot on the Billboard Hot 100, and reached number one in 17 other countries. The video, which was released on YouTube in July 2011, has been viewed more than 300 million times. In 2012, Goyte was nominated for 3 Grammy Awards, 3 Teen Choice Awards, 2 American Music Awards, and 4 MTV Europe Music Awards.

most downloaded songs
downloads in 2011, in millions

6.80	6.47	5.94	4.75	3.97
"Somebody That I Used to Know," Gotye	"Call Me Maybe," Carly Rae Jepsen	"We Are Young," fun	"Payphone," Maroon 5	"Starships," Nicki Minaj

most streamed music video

"Call Me Maybe"

Carly Rae Jepsen's smash hit "Call Me Maybe" was streamed almost 80 million times in 2012. The song, which was co-written by Jepsen and Tavish Crowe, appeared on the Canadian singer's second album, *Kiss*. The song was also included on Jepsen's 2012 album, *Curiosity*. "Call Me Maybe" reached number one on the Billboard Hot 100, and the single has sold more than 12.5 million copies worldwide. The song was nominated for two Grammy Awards—Song of the Year and Best Pop Solo Performance. MTV also named "Call Me Maybe" the song of the year in 2012.

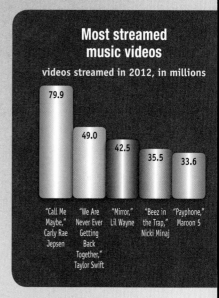

Most streamed music videos

videos streamed in 2012, in millions

"Call Me Maybe," Carly Rae Jepsen	"We Are Never Ever Getting Back Together," Taylor Swift	"Mirror," Lil Wayne	"Beez in the Trap," Nicki Minaj	"Payphone," Maroon 5
79.9	49.0	42.5	35.5	33.6

artist with the most radio airplay

Katy Perry

Katy Perry ruled the airwaves in 2012, clocking 1.39 million song detections across the country. Some of her most popular songs were from her most recent album, *Teenage Dream: The Complete Confection,* including "Wide Awake," "Part of Me," "California Gurls," "Teenage Dream," "Firework," "E.T.," and "Last Friday Night." Six of these singles also topped the Hot 100 chart. In early 2012, Perry became the first artist to have five songs sell more than 5 million copies each. Perry was also named Billboard's Woman of the Year in 2012.

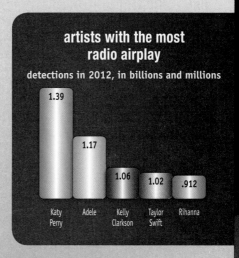

artists with the most radio airplay

detections in 2012, in billions and millions

Katy Perry	Adele	Kelly Clarkson	Taylor Swift	Rihanna
1.39	1.17	1.06	1.02	.912

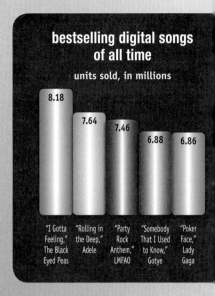

bestselling digital song of all time

"I Gotta Feeling"

The Black Eyed Peas' mega dance hit "I Gotta Feeling" is the bestselling digital song of all time with more than 8.1 million downloads. The song, which was released in May 2009, is from The Black Eyed Peas' fifth studio album, *The E.N.D.* "I Gotta Feeling" won a Grammy Award for Best Pop Performance by a Duo or Group, and was nominated for Song of the Year at the World Music Awards. The song was number one on the Billboard Hot 100 chart for 12 straight weeks and also topped music charts in 25 other countries. The members of the group are will.i.am, apl.de.ap, Taboo, and Fergie.

bestselling digital songs of all time
units sold, in millions

"I Gotta Feeling," The Black Eyed Peas	"Rolling in the Deep," Adele	"Party Rock Anthem," LMFAO	"Somebody That I Used to Know," Gotye	"Poker Face," Lady Gaga
8.18	7.64	7.46	6.88	6.86

top-earning hip-hop artist

Dr. Dre

Dr. Dre—rapper, producer, and hip-hop mogul—earned $110 million in 2012. He, along with businessman Jimmy Iovine, founded Beats by Dr. Dre in 2006. In 2008, Beats by Dr. Dre headphones were introduced and were a huge success. In mid-2011, the company was bought by mobile phone manufacturer HTC for $309 million, and Dre's share was more than $100 million. His latest song—"I Need a Doctor"—was a collaboration with Eminem in 2011, and it reached number 4 on the Billboard Hot 100. It was also nominated for two Grammys.

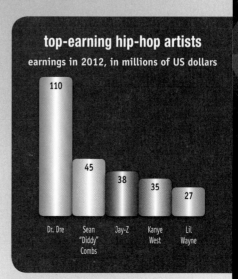

top-earning hip-hop artists

earnings in 2012, in millions of US dollars

Dr. Dre	Sean "Diddy" Combs	Jay-Z	Kanye West	Lil Wayne
110	45	38	35	27

107

bestselling album

21

Adele dominated album sales in 2012, selling more than 5.25 million copies of *21*. It was the second year that the album was number one. The album, which was named for Adele's age at the time of production, was released in January 2011. The first three singles released from the album include "Rolling in the Deep," "Someone Like You," and "Set Fire to the Rain." All three reached the top of the charts worldwide. *21* won three American Music Awards including Favorite Pop/Rock Album, Favorite Female Artist, and Adult Contemporary Artist: Favorite Artist.

bestselling albums
units sold in 2012, in millions

5.25	3.89	2.33	2.14	1.92
21, Adele	Red, Taylor Swift	Up All Night, One Direction	Believe, Justin Beiber	Some Nights, Fun

most streamed artist

Taylor Swift

Taylor Swift was the most streamed artist in 2012, with 216 million streams going out to fans. The streams, which include songs and videos, are collected from multiple Nielsen sites. Most of the 2012 streams were from Swift's last two albums, *Speak Now* from 2010, and *Red* from 2012. *Speak Now* included hits like "Mine," "Back to December," and "The Story of Us." From *Red*, Swift's most-popular tracks include "We Are Never Ever Getting Back Together," "Begin Again," and "I Knew You Were Trouble." *Red* debuted on the top of the Billboard 200 chart, and sold more than 1.2 million copies in its first week.

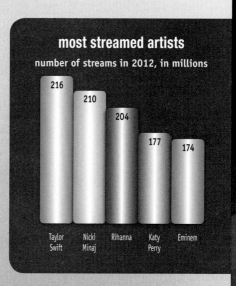

most streamed artists

number of streams in 2012, in millions

Taylor Swift	Nicki Minaj	Rihanna	Katy Perry	Eminem
216	210	204	177	174

top-earning male singer

Elton John

Music legend Elton John earned $80 million in 2012. In September 2011, John began a show at Caesar's Palace in Las Vegas entitled *The Million Dollar Piano*. The show gets its name from the pricey instrument that was created for the concert series. *Million Dollar Piano* is scheduled to run for three years. In the show, John plays about 20 songs from albums that he created over the last 40 years of his career. In July 2012, John released an album of remixed songs called *Good Morning to the Night*, and it became the first of his albums to reach number 1 on the UK charts in 22 years.

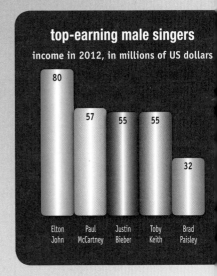

top-earning male singers
income in 2012, in millions of US dollars

Elton John	Paul McCartney	Justin Bieber	Toby Keith	Brad Paisley
80	57	55	55	32

top-earning female singer

Britney Spears

With an income of $58 million, pop sensation Britney Spears rose above the other female artists in 2012. In mid-2011, Spears released her seventh studio album, *Femme Fatale*, which debuted at number one on the US charts and has sold more than 2 million copies worldwide. The album features singles including "Hold It Against Me," "Till the World Ends," and "I Wanna Go," and each one made it into the top ten on the Billboard Hot 100. In 2012, Spears joined the cast of *The X Factor* and was paid $15 million to judge the competition's singers.

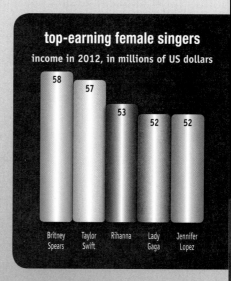

top-earning female singers
income in 2012, in millions of US dollars

Britney Spears	Taylor Swift	Rihanna	Lady Gaga	Jennifer Lopez
58	57	53	52	52

most played song

"Somebody That I Used to Know"

"Somebody That I Used to Know" by Gotye was detected more than 612,000 times on radio stations across the country during 2012. The song, which also features New Zealand singer Kimbra, was written by Gotye and has become his most successful song. It reached the top ten charts in more than 30 countries and has sold more than 10 million copies worldwide. "Somebody That I Used to Know" was released in July 2011, and Gotye has performed it on *The Voice*, *Saturday Night Live*, and *American Idol*. The song also won Single of the Year and Best Pop Release at the 2011 ARIA Music Awards in Australia—Gotye's country of residence.

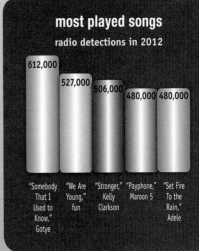

most played songs
radio detections in 2012

612,000	527,000	506,000	480,000	480,000
"Somebody That I Used to Know," Gotye	"We Are Young," fun	"Stronger," Kelly Clarkson	"Payphone," Maroon 5	"Set Fire To the Rain," Adele

musician with the most mtv video music awards

Madonna

Madonna has won 20 MTV Video Music Awards since the ceremony was first held in 1984. She has won four Cinematography awards, three Female Video awards, three Directing awards, two Editing awards, and two Art Direction awards. She also picked up single awards for Video of the Year, Choreography, Special Effects, and Long Form Video, as well as a Viewer's Choice and a Video Vanguard Award. Madonna's award-winning videos include "Papa Don't Preach," "Like a Prayer," "Express Yourself," "Vogue," "Rain," "Take a Bow," "Ray of Light," and "Beautiful Stranger."

musicians with the most mtv video music awards
awards won

Madonna	Peter Gabriel	Lady Gaga	R.E.M.	Eminem
20	13	13	12	11

113

top-earning tour

Madonna

Music veteran Madonna topped the charts of 2012, bringing in more than $296 million with her *MDNA* Tour—an average of $4.4 million per night. It also became the tenth-highest-grossing concert in history. It was the singer's ninth tour of her career and was launched to promote her twelfth studio album of the same name. Spanning from May to December 2012, the tour featured 88 shows, stopping in Asia, Europe, and North and South America. The set featured about 25 songs, mixing Madonna's new material with her classic hits.

top-earning tours
earnings in 2012, in millions of US dollars

Madonna	Bruce Springsteen	Roger Waters	Coldplay	Lady Gaga
296.1	210.2	186.4	171.3	161.4

act with the most country music awards

George Strait

George Strait has won a whopping 22 Country Music Awards and has been nicknamed the "King of Country" for all of his accomplishments in the business. He won his first CMA award in 1985, and his most recent in 2008. In addition to his many awards, Strait holds the record for the most number one hits on the Billboard Hot Country Songs with 44. He also has 38 hit albums, including 12 multiplatinum and 22 platinum records. He was inducted into the Country Music Hall of Fame in 2006.

acts with the most country music awards
awards won

George Strait	Brooks & Dunn	Vince Gill	Alan Jackson	Miranda Lambert
22	19	18	16	15

longest-running broadway show

The Phantom of the Opera

The Phantom of the Opera has been performed more than 10,368 times since it opened in January 1988. The show tells the story of a disfigured musical genius who terrorizes the performers of the Paris Opera House. More than 130 million people have seen a performance in 145 cities and 27 countries. The show won seven Tony Awards its opening year, including Best Musical. The musical drama is performed at the Majestic Theater.

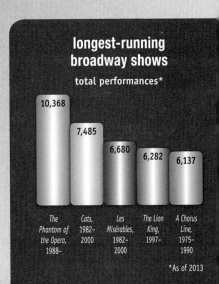

longest-running broadway shows
total performances*

The Phantom of the Opera, 1988–	Cats, 1982–2000	Les Misérables, 1982–2000	The Lion King, 1997–	A Chorus Line, 1975–1990
10,368	7,485	6,680	6,282	6,137

*As of 2013

musical with the most tony awards

The Producers

In March 2001, *The Producers* took home 12 of its record-breaking 15 Tony Award nominations. The Broadway smash won awards for Musical, Original Score, Book, Direction of a Musical, Choreography, Orchestration, Scenic Design, Costume Design, Lighting Design, Actor in a Musical, Featured Actor in a Musical, and Actress in a Musical. *The Producers*, which originally starred Nathan Lane and Matthew Broderick, is a stage adaptation of Mel Brooks's 1968 movie. Brooks wrote the lyrics and music for 16 new songs for the stage version.

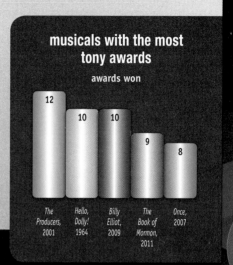

musicals with the most tony awards

awards won

The Producers, 2001	Hello, Dolly! 1964	Billy Elliot, 2009	The Book of Mormon, 2011	Once, 2007
12	10	10	9	8

117

Nature Records

Turn Down the Volume!

Cicadas are the loudest insects on earth with a chirp that can register up to 120 decibels. By comparison, any sound above 130 decibels will cause humans pain. Each species has a different song, and they can be heard up to 1.5 miles (2.4 km) away. A cicada uses a drum-like part of its abdomen called a tymbal to produce the sound.

Fish Oar Fish?

Once thought to be a sea serpent, an oar fish is really the longest bony fish that lives in the ocean. These 50-foot (15.2 m) long fish live about 3,000 feet (914.4 m) below the water's surface and are rarely seen. They have small eyes, toothless mouths, and approximately 400 dorsal fin rays on their backs.

Light Bright

One of the largest solar storms in recent history occurred in January 2012, and was intense enough to reroute flights in the polar region. Massive solar flares can also disrupt GPS readings, and disrupt satellite transmissions and power lines. Solar flares may peak in 2013, since they roughly follow an 11-year cycle.

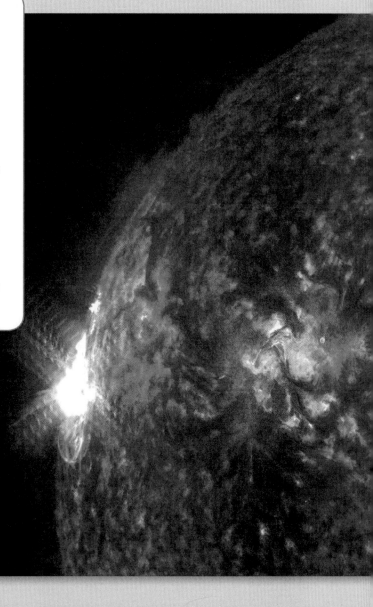

Tasty Treats

In May 2013, the United Nations encouraged people to enjoy the more than 1,900 species of insects found across the globe. While about 2 billion people worldwide already eat bugs as part of their diet, it is not common in the United States. Some species to try include stinkbugs, which have an apple flavor, and mealworms, which are high in fiber. Small grasshoppers also have as much protein as ground beef, but less fat.

Dazzling Diamonds

Earth's diamonds are billions of years old. They formed up to 120 miles (193 km) below the planet's surface at temperatures up to 3,000 degrees Fahrenheit (1,649 C). Yellow and brown diamonds are the most common, while red and blue are the rarest. Tiny bits of impurities mixed into the carbon create the color. Diamonds can be found in meteorites, but they are usually not gem quality.

Race to Recycle

The average American uses about 650 pounds (295 kg) of paper a year—the same weight as a full-grown male tiger. However, 1 ton (0.9 t) of paper made from recycled pulp saves 17 trees, 7,000 gallons (26,497 l) of water, and 3 cubic yards (202 g) of landfill space. Producing recycled white paper also creates 74 percent less air pollution than producing regular paper.

Monster Dunes

Why should sand have all the fun? In Antarctica, you can find megadunes made up of snow crystals. These dunes are about 25 feet (7.6 m) high with crests about 4 miles (6.4 km) apart. Since wind is constantly swirling, it can take several centuries to build just one dune.

largest diamond

Golden Jubilee

The Golden Jubilee is the world's largest faceted diamond, with a weight of 545.67 carats. This gigantic gem got its name when it was presented to the king of Thailand in 1997 for the Golden Jubilee—or 50th anniversary celebration—of his reign. The diamond weighed 755.5 carats when it was discovered in a South African mine in 1986. Once it was cut, the diamond featured 148 perfectly symmetrical facets. The process took almost a year because of the diamond's size and multiple tension points. The diamond is on display at the Royal Museum of Bangkok in Thailand.

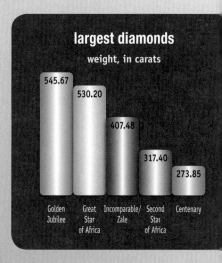

largest diamonds
weight, in carats

Golden Jubilee	Great Star of Africa	Incomparable/ Zale	Second Star of Africa	Centenary
545.67	530.20	407.48	317.40	273.85

tallest mountain

Mount Everest

Mount Everest's tallest peak towers 29,035 feet (8,850 m) into the air, and it is the highest point on Earth. This peak is an unbelievable 5.5 miles (8.8 km) above sea level. Mount Everest is located in the Himalayas, on the border between Nepal and Tibet. The mountain got its official name from surveyor Sir George Everest. In 1953, Sir Edmund Hillary and Tenzing Norgay were the first people to reach the peak. In 2008, the Olympic torch was carried up to the top of the mountain on its way to the games in Beijing.

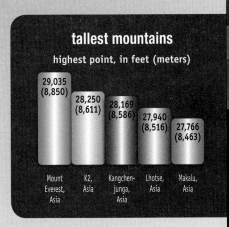

tallest mountains
highest point, in feet (meters)

29,035 (8,850)	28,250 (8,611)	28,169 (8,586)	27,940 (8,516)	27,766 (8,463)
Mount Everest, Asia	K2, Asia	Kangchen-junga, Asia	Lhotse, Asia	Makalu, Asia

123

largest lake

Caspian Sea

This giant inland body of salt water stretches for almost 750 miles (1,207 km) from north to south, with an average width of about 200 miles (322 km). Altogether, it covers 143,200 square miles (370,901 sq km). The Caspian Sea is located east of the Caucasus Mountains in central Asia. It is bordered by Iran, Russia, Kazakhstan, Azerbaijan, and Turkmenistan. The Caspian Sea has an average depth of about 550 feet (170 m). It is an important fishing resource, with species including sturgeon, salmon, perch, herring, and carp. Other animals living in the Caspian Sea include porpoises, seals, and tortoises. The sea is estimated to be 30 million years old and became landlocked 5.5 million years ago.

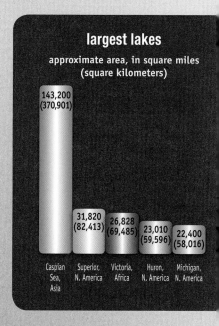

largest lakes

approximate area, in square miles
(square kilometers)

Caspian Sea, Asia	Superior, N. America	Victoria, Africa	Huron, N. America	Michigan, N. America
143,200 (370,901)	31,820 (82,413)	26,828 (69,485)	23,010 (59,596)	22,400 (58,016)

largest desert

Sahara

Located in northern Africa, the Sahara Desert covers approximately 3.5 million square miles (9.1 million sq km). It stretches for 5,200 miles (8,372 km) through the countries of Morocco, Algeria, Tunisia, Libya, Egypt, Mauritania, Mali, Niger, Chad, and Sudan. The Sahara gets very little rainfall—less than 8 inches (20 cm) per year. Even with its harsh environment, some 2.5 million people—mostly nomads—call the Sahara home. Date palms and acacias grow near oases. Some of the animals that live in the Sahara include gazelles, antelopes, jackals, foxes, and badgers.

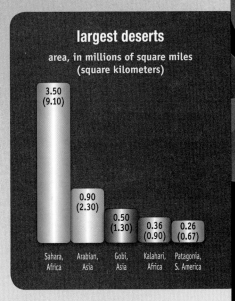

largest deserts

area, in millions of square miles (square kilometers)

Sahara, Africa	Arabian, Asia	Gobi, Asia	Kalahari, Africa	Patagonia, S. America
3.50 (9.10)	0.90 (2.30)	0.50 (1.30)	0.36 (0.90)	0.26 (0.67)

125

longest river

Nile

The Nile River in Africa stretches 4,145 miles (6,671 km) from the tributaries of Lake Victoria in Tanzania and Uganda out to the Mediterranean Sea. Because of varying depths, ships can sail on only about 2,000 miles (3,217 km) of the river. The Nile flows through Rwanda, Uganda, Sudan, and Egypt. The river's water supply is crucial to the existence of these African countries. The Nile's precious water is used to irrigate crops and to generate electricity. The Aswan Dam and the Aswan High Dam—both located in Egypt—are used to store the autumn floodwater for later use. The Nile is also used to transport goods from city to city along the river.

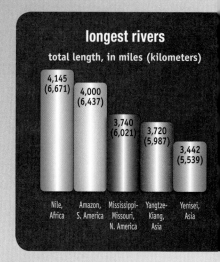

longest rivers

total length, in miles (kilometers)

Nile, Africa	Amazon, S. America	Mississippi-Missouri, N. America	Yangtze-Kiang, Asia	Yenisei, Asia
4,145 (6,671)	4,000 (6,437)	3,740 (6,021)	3,720 (5,987)	3,442 (5,539)

largest ocean

Pacific

The Pacific Ocean covers almost 64 million square miles (166 million sq km) and reaches 36,200 feet (11,000 m) below sea level at its greatest depth—the Mariana Trench (near the Philippines). In fact, this ocean is so large that it covers about one-third of the planet (more than all of Earth's land put together) and holds more than half of all the seawater on Earth. The United States could fit inside this ocean 18 times! Some of the major bodies of water included in the Pacific are the Bering Sea, the Coral Sea, the Philippine Sea, and the Gulf of Alaska.

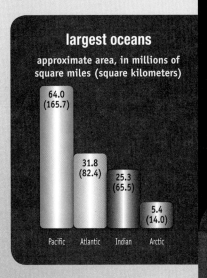

largest oceans

approximate area, in millions of square miles (square kilometers)

64.0 (165.7) — Pacific
31.8 (82.4) — Atlantic
25.3 (65.5) — Indian
5.4 (14.0) — Arctic

world's largest coral reef

Great Barrier Reef

The Great Barrier Reef stretches for some 1,429 miles (2,300 km) in the Coral Sea along the coast of Australia. It's larger than the Great Wall of China, and it's the only living thing that can be seen from space. More than 3,000 individual reef systems and coral cays make up this intricate structure. A large part of the reef makes up Great Barrier Reef Marine Park, which helps to preserve the area by limiting fishing, tourism, and human use. Thousands of animal species are supported by the reef, including 600 species of fish, 450 species of hard coral, and about 30 species of dolphins and whales. The Great Barrier Reef is considered a World Heritage Site, and one of the Seven Natural Wonders of the World.

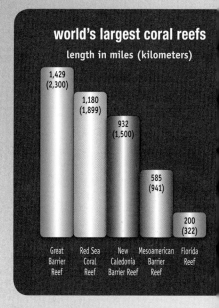

world's largest coral reefs

length in miles (kilometers)

Reef	Length in miles (kilometers)
Great Barrier Reef	1,429 (2,300)
Red Sea Coral Reef	1,180 (1,899)
New Caledonia Barrier Reef	932 (1,500)
Mesoamerican Barrier Reef	585 (941)
Florida Reef	200 (322)

world's deepest sea trench

Mariana Trench

Located in the Pacific Ocean near Japan, the Mariana Trench is the deepest opening in Earth's crust at 35,787 feet (10,907 m)—that's almost 7 miles (11.2 km). Mount Everest—the world's tallest mountain at 29,035 feet (8,850 m)—could easily fit inside. The deepest point in the trench is called the Challenger Deep, named after oceanographer Jacques Piccard's exploration vessel, which first mapped the location in 1951. The trench is home to many types of crabs and fish, as well as more than 200 different types of microorganisms.

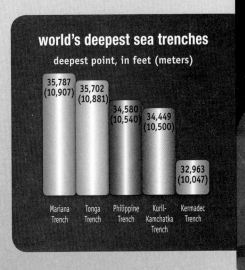

world's deepest sea trenches

deepest point, in feet (meters)

Mariana Trench	Tonga Trench	Philippine Trench	Kuril-Kamchatka Trench	Kermadec Trench
35,787 (10,907)	35,702 (10,881)	34,580 (10,540)	34,449 (10,500)	32,963 (10,047)

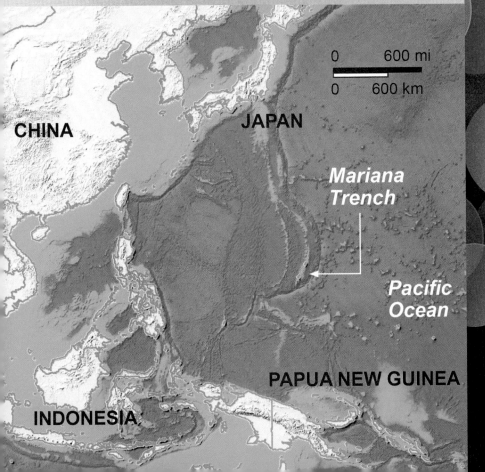

0   600 mi

0   600 km

CHINA

JAPAN

Mariana Trench

Pacific Ocean

PAPUA NEW GUINEA

INDONESIA

largest crustacean

Giant Spider Crab

The giant spider crab has a 12-foot (3.7 m) leg span. That's almost wide enough to take up two parking spaces! The crab's body measures about 15 inches (38.1 cm) wide. Its ten long legs are jointed, and the first pair has large claws at the end. The giant sea creature can weigh 35–44 pounds (16–20 kg). It feeds on dead animals and shellfish it finds on the ocean floor. Giant spider crabs live in the deep water of the Pacific Ocean off southern Japan.

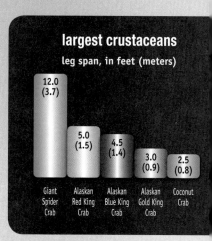

largest crustaceans
leg span, in feet (meters)

12.0 (3.7)	5.0 (1.5)	4.5 (1.4)	3.0 (0.9)	2.5 (0.8)
Giant Spider Crab	Alaskan Red King Crab	Alaskan Blue King Crab	Alaskan Gold King Crab	Coconut Crab

largest cephalopod

Colossal Squid

Living up to 6,000 feet (1,829 m) deep in the Antarctic Ocean, the colossal squid can grow to a length of 46 feet (14 m). That's about the same size as three SUVs! The squid, which is very rarely seen by people, can weigh about 1,500 pounds (681 kg). Its eyes are the size of dinner plates, and are the largest eyes in the animal kingdom. The colossal squid uses its 20-foot (6 m) long tentacles to catch its prey. In addition to the two tentacles, this giant cephalopod has eight arms. In the center of its body, the squid has a razor-sharp beak that it uses to shred its prey before eating it.

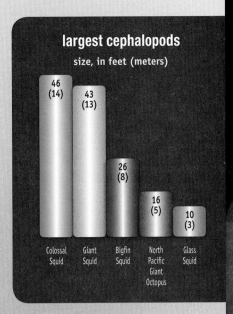

largest cephalopods

size, in feet (meters)

Colossal Squid	Giant Squid	Bigfin Squid	North Pacific Giant Octopus	Glass Squid
46 (14)	43 (13)	26 (8)	16 (5)	10 (3)

131

most dangerous shark

Great White

With a total of 249 known unprovoked attacks on humans, great white sharks are the most dangerous predators in the sea. A great white can measure more than 20 feet (6.1 m) in length and weigh up to 3,800 pounds (1,723 kg). Because of the sharks' size, they can feed on large prey, including seals, dolphins, and even small whales. Often, when a human is attacked by a great white, it is because the shark has mistaken the person for its typical prey. The sharks make their homes in most waters throughout the world, but are most frequently found off the coasts of Australia, South Africa, California, and Mexico.

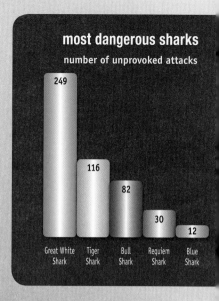

most dangerous sharks
number of unprovoked attacks

Great White Shark	Tiger Shark	Bull Shark	Requiem Shark	Blue Shark
249	116	82	30	12

biggest fish

Whale Shark

Although the average length of a whale shark is 30 feet (9 m), many have been known to reach up to 60 feet (18 m) long. That's the same length as two school buses! Whale sharks also weigh an average of 50,000 pounds (22,680 kg). As with most sharks, the females are larger than the males. Their mouths measure about 5 feet (1.5 m) long and contain about 3,000 teeth. Amazingly, these gigantic fish eat only microscopic plankton and tiny fish. They float near the surface looking for food.

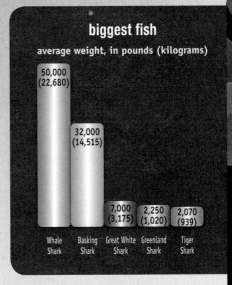

biggest fish

average weight, in pounds (kilograms)

Whale Shark	Basking Shark	Great White Shark	Greenland Shark	Tiger Shark
50,000 (22,680)	32,000 (14,515)	7,000 (3,175)	2,250 (1,020)	2,070 (939)

fastest fish

Sailfish

A sailfish once grabbed a fishing line and dragged it 300 feet (91 m) away in just three seconds. That means it was swimming at an average speed of 69 miles (109 km) per hour—higher than the average speed limit on a highway! Sailfish are very large—they average 6 feet (1.8 m) long, but can grow up to 11 feet (3.4 m). They eat squid and surface-dwelling fish, and sometimes several sailfish will work together to catch their prey. They are found in both the Atlantic and Pacific oceans and prefer a water temperature of about 80°F (27°C).

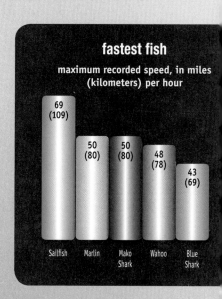

fastest fish

maximum recorded speed, in miles (kilometers) per hour

Sailfish	Martin	Mako Shark	Wahoo	Blue Shark
69 (109)	50 (80)	50 (80)	48 (78)	43 (69)

biggest dolphin

Orca

Although they are known as *killer whales*, the orca is actually a member of the dolphin family and can measure up to 32 feet (9.7 m) in length and weigh up to 6 tons (5.4 t). These powerful marine mammals are carnivores with 4-inch (1.6 cm) long teeth, and they feed mainly on seals, sea lions, and smaller whales. Orcas live in pods of up to 40 other whales, and pod members help one another round up prey. Killer whales can live for up to 80 years and are highly intelligent. Trainers in aquariums often work with orcas to perform live shows.

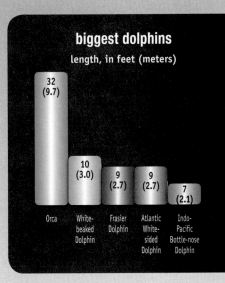

biggest dolphins

length, in feet (meters)

32 (9.7)	10 (3.0)	9 (2.7)	9 (2.7)	7 (2.1)
Orca	White-beaked Dolphin	Frasier Dolphin	Atlantic White-sided Dolphin	Indo-Pacific Bottle-nose Dolphin

heaviest marine mammal

Blue Whale

Blue whales are the largest animals that have ever inhabited Earth. They can weigh more than 143.3 tons (130 t) and measure over 100 feet (30 m) long. Amazingly, these gentle giants only eat krill—small shrimplike animals. A blue whale can eat about 4 tons (3.6 t) of krill each day in the summer, when food is plentiful. To catch the krill, a whale gulps as much as 17,000 gallons (64,600 L) of seawater into its mouth at one time. Then it uses its tongue—which can be as big as a car—to push the water back out. The krill get caught in hairs on the whale's baleen (a keratin filtering structure that hangs down from the roof of the whale's mouth).

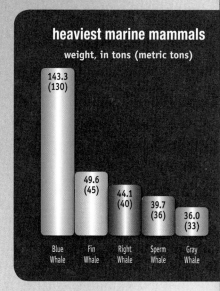

heaviest marine mammals
weight, in tons (metric tons)

Blue Whale	Fin Whale	Right Whale	Sperm Whale	Gray Whale
143.3 (130)	49.6 (45)	44.1 (40)	39.7 (36)	36.0 (33)

marine mammal with the largest brain

Sperm Whale

The sperm whale's brain is the largest marine mammal brain in the world, weighing more than 17 pounds (7.7 kg). That's more than five times the size of a human brain. Sperm whales can grow to about 60 feet (18 m) long and weigh up to 45 tons (41 t). The head makes up about one-third of the animal's body. Sperm whales can also dive deeper than any other whale, reaching depths of 3,300 feet (1,006 m) in search of squid. They can eat about 1 ton (0.9 t) of fish and squid daily. Sperm whales can be found in all oceans, and they generally live in pods of about a dozen adults and their offspring.

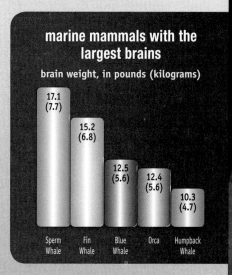

marine mammals with the largest brains

brain weight, in pounds (kilograms)

Sperm Whale	Fin Whale	Blue Whale	Orca	Humpback Whale
17.1 (7.7)	15.2 (6.8)	12.5 (5.6)	12.4 (5.6)	10.3 (4.7)

largest bird wingspan

Marabou Stork

With a wingspan that can reach up to 13 feet (4 m), the marabou stork has the largest wingspan of any bird. These large storks weigh up to 20 pounds (9 kg) and can grow up to 5 feet (150 cm) tall. Their long leg bones and toe bones are actually hollow. This adaptation is very important for flight because it makes the bird lighter. Although marabous eat insects, small mammals, and fish, the majority of their food is carrion—meat that is already dead. In fact, the stork's head and neck do not have any feathers. This helps the bird stay clean as it sticks its head into carcasses to pick out scraps of food.

largest bird wingspans

wingspan, in feet (meters)

Marabou Stork	Albatross	Trumpeter Swan	Mute Swan	Whooper Swan
13 (4.0)	12 (3.7)	11 (3.4)	10 (3.0)	10 (3.0)

biggest penguin

Emperor Penguin

Emperor penguins are giants among their species, growing to a height of 44 inches (111.7 cm) and weighing up to 80 pounds (37 kg). These penguins are the only animals that spend the entire winter on the open ice in Antarctica, withstanding temperatures as low as -75°F (-60°C). The female penguin lays a 1-pound (0.5 kg) egg on the ice, and then goes off to hunt for weeks at a time. The male penguin scoops up the egg, and keeps it warm on his feet below his toasty belly. When the eggs hatch, the females return with food.

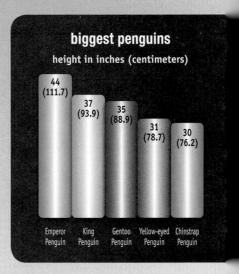

biggest penguins
height in inches (centimeters)

Emperor Penguin	King Penguin	Gentoo Penguin	Yellow-eyed Penguin	Chinstrap Penguin
44 (111.7)	37 (93.9)	35 (88.9)	31 (78.7)	30 (76.2)

world's largest owl

Blakiston's Fish Owl

A female Blakiston's fish owl can measure up to 3 feet (.9 m) high, weigh up to 10 pounds (4.5 kg), and have a 6-foot (1.8 m) wingspan. Females are larger than males. As its name suggests, the Blakiston's fish owl primarily eats fish—including pike, trout, and salmon—and can catch a meal that weighs almost as much as the owl itself. These birds live and nest in old-growth forests along coastlines throughout Japan and Russia. However, due to forest clearing and other threats to its habitat, the Blakiston's fish owl is endangered.

some of the world's largest owls

weight in pounds (kilograms)

Blakiston's Fish Owl	Eurasian Eagle Owl	Snowy Owl	Great Horned Owl	Great Grey Owl
10 (4.5)	9 (4.1)	6.5 (2.9)	5.5 (2.5)	3.8 (1.7)

A pair of juvenile bald eagles near their nest

bird that builds the largest nest

Bald Eagle

With a nest that can measure 8 feet (2.4 m) wide and 16 feet (4.9 m) deep, bald eagles have plenty of room to move around. These birds of prey have wingspans of up to 7.5 feet (2.3 m) and need a home that they can nest in comfortably. By carefully constructing their nest with sticks, branches, and plant material, a pair of bald eagles can balance their home—which can weigh up to 4,000 pounds (1,814 kg)—on the top of a tree or cliff. These nests are usually located by rivers or coastlines, the birds' watery hunting grounds. Called an aerie, this home will be used for the rest of the eagles' lives.

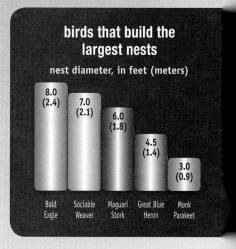

birds that build the largest nests

nest diameter, in feet (meters)

Bald Eagle	Sociable Weaver	Maguari Stork	Great Blue Heron	Monk Parakeet
8.0 (2.4)	7.0 (2.1)	6.0 (1.8)	4.5 (1.4)	3.0 (0.9)

largest bird egg

Ostrich Egg

Ostriches—the world's largest birds—can lay eggs that measure 5 inches by 6 inches (13 cm by 16 cm) and weigh up to 4 pounds (1.8 kg). In fact, just one ostrich egg weighs as much as 24 chicken eggs! The egg yolk makes up one-third of the volume. Although the eggshell is only 0.08 inches (2 mm) thick, it is tough enough to withstand the weight of a 345-pound (157 kg) ostrich. An ostrich hen can lay from 10 to 70 eggs each year. Females are usually able to recognize their own eggs, even when they are mixed in with those of other females in their shared nest.

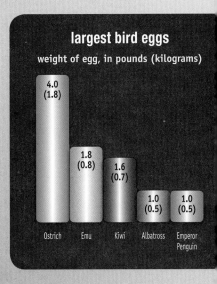

largest bird eggs
weight of egg, in pounds (kilograms)

Ostrich	Emu	Kiwi	Albatross	Emperor Penguin
4.0 (1.8)	1.8 (0.8)	1.6 (0.7)	1.0 (0.5)	1.0 (0.5)

Sockeye salmon

most endangered US animal group

Fish

There are 83 species of fish that are currently endangered in the United States. A species is considered endangered if it is in danger of becoming extinct. In addition, there are another 70 fish species that are considered threatened. Out of the 153 endangered and threatened fish species, there is a recovery plan in place for 102 of them. The main reasons for the decline in some species' populations are overfishing, water pollution, and loss of habitat. Some of the most well-known endangered fish include the Atlantic salmon, the steelhead trout, the sockeye salmon, and the Atlantic sturgeon.

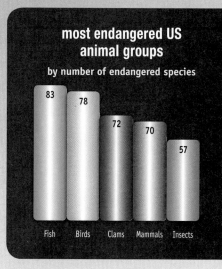

most endangered US animal groups
by number of endangered species

Fish	Birds	Clams	Mammals	Insects
83	78	72	70	57

biggest bear

Polar Bear

A massive male polar bear can weigh in at up to 1,600 pounds (726 kg), which is about the same weight as ten grown men. Females are smaller than the males, and the weight of both genders fluctuates when food is scarce. The 8-foot (2.4 m) tall animals live in the frigid Arctic, patrolling the ice and surrounding water for food. Polar bears are excellent swimmers, and can travel more than 100 miles (161 km) in icy water searching for seals to eat. Their dense coats protect them from snow, ice, and wind. They even have thick strips of fur on their paws to insulate their feet and help them grip the ice.

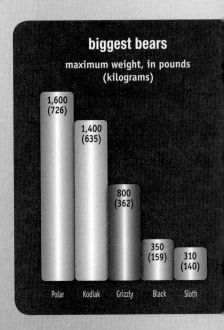

biggest bears
maximum weight, in pounds (kilograms)

Polar	Kodiak	Grizzly	Black	Sloth
1,600 (726)	1,400 (635)	800 (362)	350 (159)	310 (140)

heaviest land mammal

African Elephant

Weighing in at up to 14,430 pounds (6,545 kg) and measuring approximately 24 feet (7.3 m) long, African elephants are truly humongous. Even at their great size, they are strictly vegetarian. They will, however, eat up to 500 pounds (226 kg) of vegetation a day! Their two tusks—which are actually elongated teeth—grow continuously during their lives and can reach about 9 feet (2.7 m) in length. Elephants live in small groups of 8 to 15 family members with one female (called a cow) as the leader.

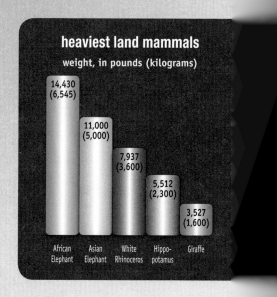

heaviest land mammals
weight, in pounds (kilograms)

	Weight
African Elephant	14,430 (6,545)
Asian Elephant	11,000 (5,000)
White Rhinoceros	7,937 (3,600)
Hippopotamus	5,512 (2,300)
Giraffe	3,527 (1,600)

largest rodent

Capybara

Capybaras reach an average length of 4 feet (1.2 m), stand about 20 inches (51 cm) tall, and weigh 75–150 pounds (34–68 kg)! That's about the same size as a Labrador retriever. Also known as water hogs and carpinchos, capybaras are found in South and Central America, where they spend much of their time in groups, looking for food. They are strictly vegetarian and have been known to raid gardens for melons and squash. Their partially webbed feet make capybaras excellent swimmers. They can dive down to the bottom of a lake or river to find plants and stay there for up to five minutes.

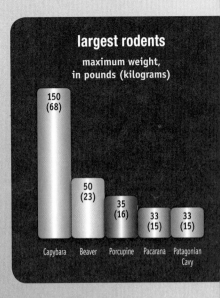

largest rodents

maximum weight,
in pounds (kilograms)

Capybara	Beaver	Porcupine	Pacarana	Patagonian Cavy
150 (68)	50 (23)	35 (16)	33 (15)	33 (15)

biggest wolf

Arctic Wolf

The gray wolf is the largest member of the Canidae family, which also includes foxes, coyotes, jackals, and dogs. There are five subspecies of the gray wolf, and of them, the Arctic wolf is the largest. Measuring 32 inches (81 cm) long and weighing up to 175 pounds (79 kg), these meat-eating mammals live and hunt in packs. Working together, they can take down prey much larger than themselves, including deer, moose, and caribou. Gray wolves can chase prey for more than 20 minutes, sometimes reaching speeds of 35 miles (56 km) per hour. They live throughout North America and in parts of Europe and Asia.

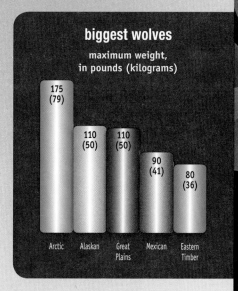

biggest wolves

maximum weight,
in pounds (kilograms)

Arctic	Alaskan	Great Plains	Mexican	Eastern Timber
175 (79)	110 (50)	110 (50)	90 (41)	80 (36)

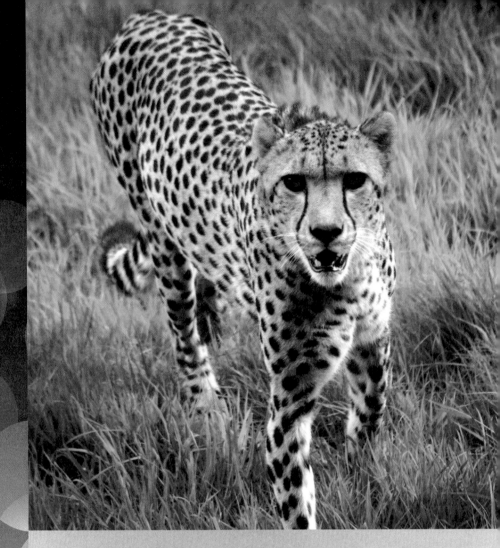

fastest land mammal

Cheetah

For short spurts, these sleek mammals can reach a speed of 71 miles (114 km) per hour. They can accelerate from 0 to 40 miles (64 km) per hour in just three strides. Their quickness easily enables these large African cats to outrun their prey. All other African cats can only stalk their prey because they lack the cheetah's amazing speed. Unlike the paws of all other cats, cheetah paws do not have skin sheaths (thin protective coverings). Their claws, therefore, cannot be retracted.

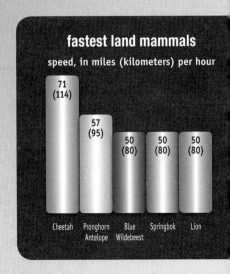

fastest land mammals
speed, in miles (kilometers) per hour

Cheetah	Pronghorn Antelope	Blue Wildebeest	Springbok	Lion
71 (114)	57 (95)	50 (80)	50 (80)	50 (80)

world's heaviest cat

Tiger

Although tigers average about 448 pounds (203 kg), some of these big cats can grow to 725 pounds (328 kg) and measure 6 feet (1.8 m) long—not including a 3-foot (0.9 m) tail. Tigers that live in colder habitats are usually larger than ones that live in warmer areas. These giant cats hunt at night, and can easily bring down a full-grown antelope alone. One tiger can eat about 60 pounds (27 kg) of meat in just one night. The five types of tigers are Bengal, Indochinese, South China, Sumatran, and Siberian. All tiger species are endangered, mostly because of over-hunting and loss of habitat due to farming and logging.

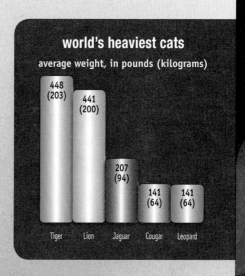

world's heaviest cats
average weight, in pounds (kilograms)

Tiger	Lion	Jaguar	Cougar	Leopard
448 (203)	441 (200)	207 (94)	141 (64)	141 (64)

largest bat

Giant Flying Fox

The giant flying fox—a member of the megabat family—can have a wingspan of up to 6 feet (1.8 m). These furry mammals average just 7 wing beats per second, but can travel more than 40 miles (64 km) a night in search of food. Unlike smaller bats, which use echolocation, flying foxes rely on their acute vision and sense of smell to locate fruit, pollen, and nectar. Flying foxes got their name because their faces resemble a fox's face. Megabats live in the tropical areas of Africa, Asia, and Australia.

150

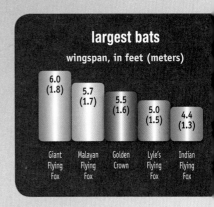

largest bats

wingspan, in feet (meters)

6.0 (1.8)	5.7 (1.7)	5.5 (1.6)	5.0 (1.5)	4.4 (1.3)
Giant Flying Fox	Malayan Flying Fox	Golden Crown	Lyle's Flying Fox	Indian Flying Fox

tallest land animal

Giraffe

Giraffes are the giants among mammals, growing up to 18 feet (5.5 m) in height. That means an average giraffe could look through the window of a two-story building! A giraffe's neck is 18 times longer than a human's, but both mammals have exactly the same number of neck bones. A giraffe's long legs enable it to outrun most of its enemies. When cornered, a giraffe's long legs have the strength to kill a lion with a single kick to the head.

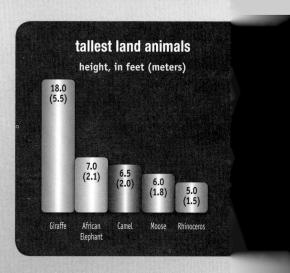

tallest land animals
height, in feet (meters)

Giraffe	African Elephant	Camel	Moose	Rhinoceros
18.0 (5.5)	7.0 (2.1)	6.5 (2.0)	6.0 (1.8)	5.0 (1.5)

world's largest domestic rabbit

Flemish Giant

The Flemish giant rabbit can weigh up to 20 pounds (9 kg) and measure about 2.5 feet (.7 m) long—about two and a half times the size of the average house cat. These rabbits are believed to have been first bred in Belgium in the 16th century, mostly for their meat and fur. In the early 20th century, Flemish giants became very popular in pet shows because of their large size and dense fur. The fur can be black, blue, fawn, light gray, sandy, steel gray, or white. Many Flemish giants are also owned as pets because they are very gentle animals. In captivity, they can live for up to ten years.

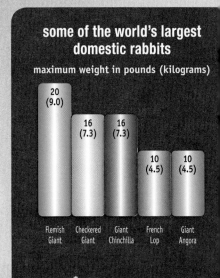

some of the world's largest domestic rabbits

maximum weight in pounds (kilograms)

Flemish Giant	Checkered Giant	Giant Chinchilla	French Lop	Giant Angora
20 (9.0)	16 (7.3)	16 (7.3)	10 (4.5)	10 (4.5)

largest primate

Gorilla

Gorillas are the kings of the primate family, weighing in at up to 400 pounds (181 kg). The eastern lowland gorilla is the largest of the four subspecies of gorillas, which also include western lowland, Cross River, and mountain. All gorillas are found in Africa, and all but mountain gorillas live in tropical forests. They are mostly plant eaters, but will occasionally eat small animals. An adult male gorilla can eat up to 45 pounds (32 kg) of food in a day. Gorillas live in groups of about 4 to 12 family members, and can live for about 35 years in the wild.

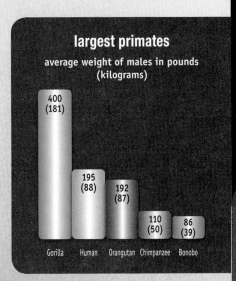

largest primates
average weight of males in pounds (kilograms)

Gorilla	Human	Orangutan	Chimpanzee	Bonobo
400 (181)	195 (88)	192 (87)	110 (50)	86 (39)

deadliest amphibian

Poison Dart Frog

Poison dart frogs are found mostly in the tropical rain forests of Central and South America, where they live on the moist land. These lethal amphibians have enough poison to kill up to 20 humans. A dart frog's poison is so effective that native Central and South Americans sometimes coat their hunting arrows or hunting darts with it. These brightly colored frogs can be yellow, orange, red, green, blue, or any combination of these colors. They measure only 0.5–2 inches (1–5 cm) long. There are approximately 75 different species of poison dart frogs.

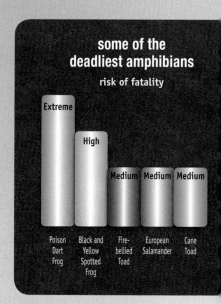

some of the deadliest amphibians
risk of fatality

Extreme	High	Medium	Medium	Medium
Poison Dart Frog	Black and Yellow Spotted Frog	Fire-bellied Toad	European Salamander	Cane Toad

longest snake

Reticulated Python

Some adult reticulated pythons can grow to 27 feet (8.2 m) long, but most reach an average length of 17 feet (5 m). That's almost the length of an average school bus! These pythons live mostly in Asia, from Myanmar to Indonesia to the Philippines. Pythons have teeth that curl backward to hold their prey, and they hunt mainly at night for mammals and birds. Reticulated pythons are slow-moving creatures that kill their prey by constriction, or strangulation.

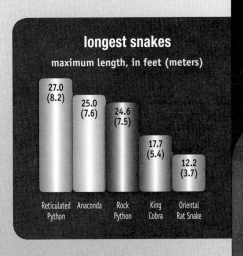

longest snakes

maximum length, in feet (meters)

27.0 (8.2)	25.0 (7.6)	24.6 (7.5)	17.7 (5.4)	12.2 (3.7)
Reticulated Python	Anaconda	Rock Python	King Cobra	Oriental Rat Snake

snake with the longest fangs

Gaboon Viper

The fangs of a Gaboon viper measure 2 inches (5.1 cm) in length! These giant fangs fold up against the snake's mouth so it does not pierce its own skin. When it is ready to strike its prey, the fangs snap down into position. The snake can grow up to 7 feet (2 m) long and weigh 18 pounds (8 kg). It is found in Africa and is perfectly camouflaged for hunting on the ground beneath leaves and grasses. The Gaboon viper's poison is not as toxic as some other snakes', but it is quite dangerous because of the amount of poison it can inject at one time. The snake is not very aggressive, however, and usually attacks only when bothered.

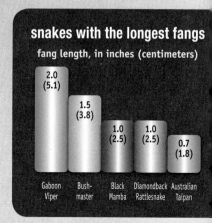

snakes with the longest fangs

fang length, in inches (centimeters)

Gaboon Viper	Bush-master	Black Mamba	Diamondback Rattlesnake	Australian Taipan
2.0 (5.1)	1.5 (3.8)	1.0 (2.5)	1.0 (2.5)	0.7 (1.8)

country with the most reptile species

Australia

There are at least 987 reptile species living throughout the continent of Australia. Lizards account for the most with 737 species, followed by snakes with more than 200 different species. Australia also has more species of venomous snakes than any other continent. Among the deadliest Australian snakes are the common death adder, the lowlands copperhead, and several types of taipans. Many reptiles thrive in the hot, dry desert climate of Australia. The world's largest reptile—the saltwater crocodile—is also found there. Some of the other well-known reptile residents include sea and freshwater turtles, which nest and lay eggs along Australia's shoreline.

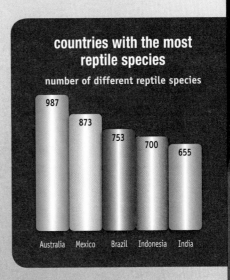

countries with the most reptile species

number of different reptile species

Australia	Mexico	Brazil	Indonesia	India
987	873	753	700	655

Australia frilled lizard

157

largest amphibian

Chinese Giant Salamander

With a length of 6 feet (1.8 m) and a weight of 55 pounds (25 kg), Chinese giant salamanders rule the amphibian world. This salamander has a large head, but its eyes and nostrils are small. It has short legs, a long tail, and very smooth skin. This large creature can be found in the streams of northeastern, central, and southern China. It feeds on fish, frogs, crabs, and snakes. The Chinese giant salamander will not hunt its prey. It waits until a potential meal wanders too close and then grabs it in its mouth. Because many people enjoy the taste of the salamander's meat, it is often hunted and its population is shrinking.

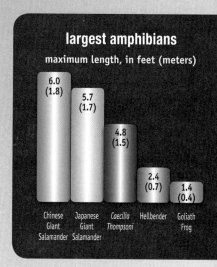

largest amphibians
maximum length, in feet (meters)

Chinese Giant Salamander	Japanese Giant Salamander	*Caecilia Thompsoni*	Hellbender	Goliath Frog
6.0 (1.8)	5.7 (1.7)	4.8 (1.5)	2.4 (0.7)	1.4 (0.4)

largest frog

Goliath Frog

The Goliath frog has a body that measures 13 inches (33 cm) long, but when its legs are extended, its total body length can increase to more than 2.5 feet (0.76 m). These gigantic frogs can weigh around 7 pounds (3 kg). Oddly enough, the eggs and tadpoles of this species are the same size as smaller frogs'. Goliath frogs are found only in the western African countries of Equatorial Guinea and Cameroon. They live in rivers that are surrounded by dense rain forests. These huge amphibians are becoming endangered, mostly because their rain forest homes are being destroyed.

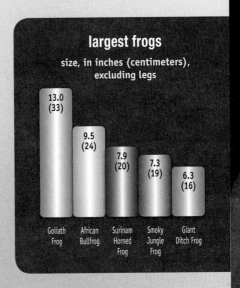

largest frogs

size, in inches (centimeters), excluding legs

Goliath Frog	African Bullfrog	Surinam Horned Frog	Smoky Jungle Frog	Giant Ditch Frog
13.0 (33)	9.5 (24)	7.9 (20)	7.3 (19)	6.3 (16)

largest lizard

Komodo Dragon

With a length of 10 feet (3 m) and a weight of 300 pounds (136 kg), Komodo dragons are the largest lizards roaming the earth. A Komodo dragon has a long neck and tail, and strong legs. These members of the monitor family are found mainly on Komodo Island, located in the Lesser Sunda Islands of Indonesia. Komodos are dangerous and have even been known to attack and kill humans. A Komodo uses its sense of smell to locate food, using its long, yellow tongue. A Komodo can consume 80 percent of its body weight in just one meal!

largest lizards

length, in feet (meters)

Komodo Dragon	Water Monitor	Perentie	Common Iguana	Marine Iguana
10.0 (3.0)	8.8 (2.7)	7.8 (2.4)	5.0 (1.5)	5.0 (1.5)

largest reptile

Saltwater Crocodile

Saltwater crocodiles can grow to 22 feet (6.7 m) long. That's about twice the length of the average car! However, males usually measure only about 17 feet (5 m) long, and females normally reach about 10 feet (3 m) in length. A large adult will feed on buffalo, monkeys, cattle, wild boar, and other large mammals. Saltwater crocodiles are found throughout the East Indies and Australia. Despite their name, saltwater crocodiles can also be found in freshwater and swamps. Some other common names for this species are the estuarine crocodile and the Indo-Pacific crocodile.

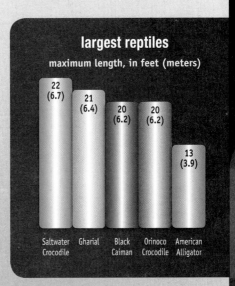

largest reptiles

maximum length, in feet (meters)

Saltwater Crocodile	Gharial	Black Caiman	Orinoco Crocodile	American Alligator
22 (6.7)	21 (6.4)	20 (6.2)	20 (6.2)	13 (3.9)

Goliath Birdeater

A Goliath birdeater is about the same size as a dinner plate—it can grow to a total length of 11 inches (28 cm) and weigh about 6 ounces (170 g). A Goliath's spiderlings are also big—they can have a 6-inch (15 cm) leg span just one year after hatching. These giant tarantulas are found mostly in the rain forests of Guyana, Suriname, Brazil, and Venezuela. The Goliath birdeater's name is misleading—they commonly eat insects and small reptiles. Similar to other tarantula species, the Goliath birdeater lives in a burrow. The spider will wait by the opening to ambush prey that gets too close.

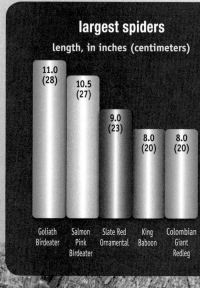

largest spiders

length, in inches (centimeters)

Goliath Birdeater	Salmon Pink Birdeater	Slate Red Ornamental	King Baboon	Colombian Giant Redleg
11.0 (28)	10.5 (27)	9.0 (23)	8.0 (20)	8.0 (20)

fastest-flying insect

Hawk Moth

The average hawk moth—which got its name from its swift and steady flight—can cruise along at speeds over 33 miles (53 km) per hour. That's faster than the average speed limit on most city streets! Although they are found throughout the world, most live in tropical climates. Also known as the sphinx moth and the hummingbird moth, this large insect can have a wingspan that reaches up to 8 inches (20 cm). Hawk moths also have good memories and may return to the same flowers at the same time each day.

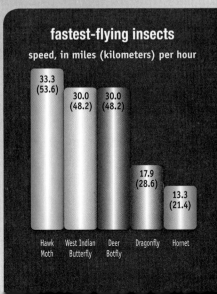

fastest-flying insects

speed, in miles (kilometers) per hour

Insect	Speed
Hawk Moth	33.3 (53.6)
West Indian Butterfly	30.0 (48.2)
Deer Botfly	30.0 (48.2)
Dragonfly	17.9 (28.6)
Hornet	13.3 (21.4)

world's most common insect

Beetle

There are more than 350,000 different types of beetles crawling around in the world. This makes up about 25 percent of all life-forms on Earth. About 40 percent of all insects are beetles. They come in all shapes, colors, and sizes. The most common types of insects in this order are weevils and rove beetles. Some of the most well-known include ladybugs, fireflies, and dung beetles. Beetles are found in all climates except cold polar regions. Fossils indicate that beetles may have been around for about 300 million years.

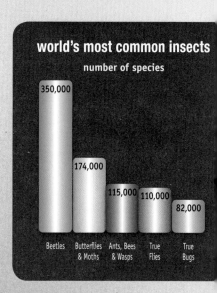

world's most common insects
number of species

Beetles	Butterflies & Moths	Ants, Bees & Wasps	True Flies	True Bugs
350,000	174,000	115,000	110,000	82,000

longest insect migration

Monarch Butterfly

Millions of monarch butterflies travel to Mexico from all parts of North America every fall, flying as far as 2,700 miles (4,345 km). Once there, they will huddle together in the trees and wait out the cold weather. In spring and summer, most butterflies only live four or five weeks as adults, but in the fall, a special generation of monarchs is born. These butterflies will live for about seven months and participate in the great migration to Mexico. Scientists are studying these butterflies in the hope of learning how the insects know where and when to migrate to a place they have never visited before.

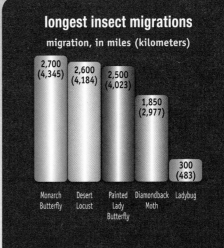

longest insect migrations

migration, in miles (kilometers)

Monarch Butterfly	Desert Locust	Painted Lady Butterfly	Diamondback Moth	Ladybug
2,700 (4,345)	2,600 (4,184)	2,500 (4,023)	1,850 (2,977)	300 (483)

Dog

More than 36.5 percent of households across the United States own one or more dogs. About 28 percent of these families own two dogs, while another 12 percent own three or more. Approximately 70 million dogs live in the country. When it comes to finding a dog, approximately 21 percent of families head to a shelter to adopt one. Those who prefer purebreds tend to choose Labrador retrievers, German shepherds, and Yorkshire terriers. Some of the most popular dog names include Bella, Max, Daisy, and Buddy.

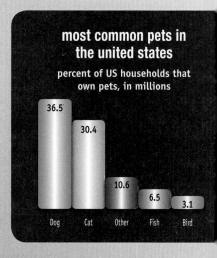

most common pets in the united states

percent of US households that own pets, in millions

Dog	Cat	Other	Fish	Bird
36.5	30.4	10.6	6.5	3.1

most popular dog breed in the united states

Labrador Retriever

Labrador retrievers are top dog in the United States! In 2012, the American Kennel Club recorded more purebred dog registrations for Labs than any other dog in the United States. Labs are very popular with families because of their gentle nature, and they are popular with hunters because of their retrieving skills. A very intelligent breed, Labrador retrievers can be trained to work in law enforcement or as guide dogs. They come in three colors—yellow, black, and brown—and are medium-size athletic dogs. They are considered by the American Kennel Club to be part of the sporting class.

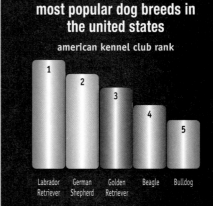

most popular dog breeds in the united states

american kennel club rank

Labrador Retriever	German Shepherd	Golden Retriever	Beagle	Bulldog
1	2	3	4	5

167

most popular cat breed in the united states

Persian

The Cat Fanciers' Association—the world's largest registry of pedigree cats—ranks the Persian as the most popular cat in the country. These flat-faced cats are known for their gentle personalities, which make them popular family pets. Persians come in many colors, including silver, golden, smoke, and tabby. They have long hair, which requires continuous grooming and maintenance. These pets, like most other cat breeds, can live as long as 15 years.

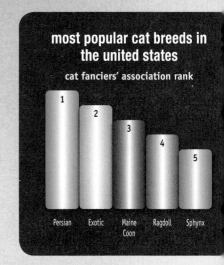

most popular cat breeds in the united states
cat fanciers' association rank

Persian	Exotic	Maine Coon	Ragdoll	Sphynx
1	2	3	4	5

united states' greatest annual snowfall

Mount Rainier

Mount Rainier had a record snowfall of 1,224 inches (3,109 cm) between February 1971 and February 1972. That's enough snow to cover a ten-story building! Located in the Cascade Mountains of Washington State, Mount Rainier is actually a volcano buried under 35 square miles (90.7 sq km) of snow and ice. The mountain, which covers about 100 square miles (259 sq km), reaches a height of 14,410 feet (4,392 m). Its three peaks include Liberty Cap, Point Success, and Columbia Crest. Mount Rainier National Park was established in 1899.

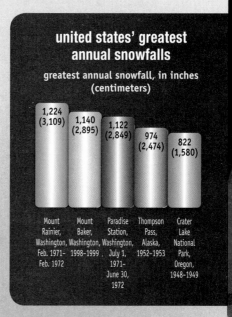

united states' greatest annual snowfalls

greatest annual snowfall, in inches (centimeters)

1,224 (3,109)	1,140 (2,895)	1,122 (2,849)	974 (2,474)	822 (1,580)
Mount Rainier, Washington, Feb. 1971– Feb. 1972	Mount Baker, Washington, 1998–1999	Paradise Station, Washington, July 1, 1971– June 30, 1972	Thompson Pass, Alaska, 1952–1953	Crater Lake National Park, Oregon, 1948–1949

coldest inhabited place

Resolute

The residents of Resolute, Canada, have to bundle up—the average temperature is just -11.6°F (-24.2°C). Located on the northeast shore of Resolute Bay on the south coast of Cornwallis Island, the community is commonly the starting point for expeditions to the North Pole. In the winter it can stay dark for 24 hours, and in the summer it can stay light during the entire night. Only about 200 people brave the climate year-round, but the area is becoming quite popular with tourists.

coldest inhabited places

average temperature, in degrees fahrenheit (celsius)

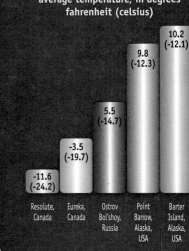

Resolute, Canada	Eureka, Canada	Ostrov Bol'shoy, Russia	Point Barrow, Alaska, USA	Barter Island, Alaska, USA
-11.6 (-24.2)	-3.5 (-19.7)	5.5 (-14.7)	9.8 (-12.3)	10.2 (-12.1)

hottest inhabited place

Dallol

Throughout the year, temperatures in Dallol, Ethiopia, average 93.2°F (34°C). Dallol is at the northernmost tip of the Great Rift Valley. The Dallol Depression reaches 328 feet (100 m) below sea level, making it the lowest point below sea level that is not covered by water. The area also has several active volcanoes. The only people to inhabit the region are the Afar, who have adapted to the harsh conditions there. For instance, to collect water, the women build covered stone piles and wait for condensation to form on the rocks.

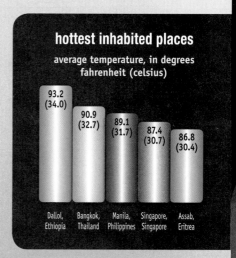

hottest inhabited places

average temperature, in degrees fahrenheit (celsius)

93.2 (34.0)	90.9 (32.7)	89.1 (31.7)	87.4 (30.7)	86.8 (30.4)
Dallol, Ethiopia	Bangkok, Thailand	Manila, Philippines	Singapore, Singapore	Assab, Eritrea

wettest inhabited place

Lloro

Umbrellas are in constant use in Lloro, Colombia, where the average annual rainfall totals about 524 inches (1,328 cm). That's about 1.4 inches (3.5 cm) a day, totaling more than 43 feet (13 m) a year! Located in the northwestern part of the country, Lloro is near the Pacific Ocean and the Caribbean Sea. Trade winds help bring lots of moisture from the coasts to this tropical little town, creating the humidity and precipitation that soak this lowland. Lloro is home to about 7,000 people.

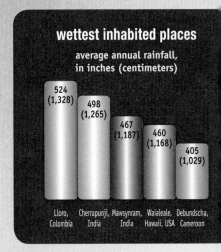

wettest inhabited places
average annual rainfall, in inches (centimeters)

Lloro, Colombia	Cherrapunji, India	Mawsynram, India	Waialeale, Hawaii, USA	Debundscha, Cameroon
524 (1,328)	498 (1,265)	467 (1,187)	460 (1,168)	405 (1,029)

driest inhabited place

Aswan

Each year, only 0.02 inches (0.5 mm) of rain falls on Aswan, Egypt. In the country's sunniest and southernmost city, summer temperatures can reach a blistering 114°F (46°C). Aswan is located on the west bank of the Nile River, and it has a very busy marketplace that is also popular with tourists. The Aswan High Dam, at 12,565 feet (3,830 m) long, is the city's most famous landmark. It produces the majority of Egypt's power in the form of hydroelectricity.

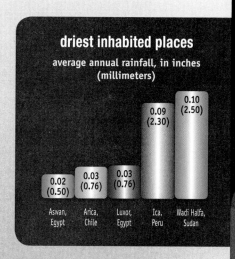

driest inhabited places
average annual rainfall, in inches (millimeters)

Aswan, Egypt	Arica, Chile	Luxor, Egypt	Ica, Peru	Wadi Halfa, Sudan
0.02 (0.50)	0.03 (0.76)	0.03 (0.76)	0.09 (2.30)	0.10 (2.50)

Barrow Island

On April 12, 1996, Cyclone Olivia blew through Barrow Island in Australia and created a wind gust that reached 253 miles (407 km) an hour. Barrow Island is about 30 miles (48 km) off the coast of Western Australia and is home to many endangered species, such as dugongs and green turtles. The dry, sandy land measures about 78 square miles (202 sq km) and is the second-largest island in Western Australia. Barrow Island also has hundreds of oil wells and is a top source of oil for the country. The island has produced more than 300 million barrels of oil since 1967.

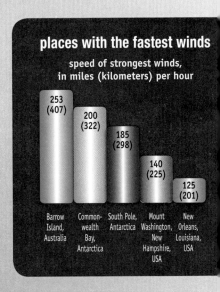

places with the fastest winds

speed of strongest winds, in miles (kilometers) per hour

253 (407)	200 (322)	185 (298)	140 (225)	125 (201)
Barrow Island, Australia	Common-wealth Bay, Antarctica	South Pole, Antarctica	Mount Washington, New Hampshire, USA	New Orleans, Louisiana, USA

tallest cactus

Saguaro

Many saguaro cacti grow to a height of 50 feet (15 m), but some have actually reached 75 feet (23 m). That's taller than a seven-story building! Saguaros start out quite small and grow very slowly. A saguaro reaches only about 1 inch (2.5 cm) high during its first 10 years. It will not bloom until it is between 50 and 75 years old. By this time, the cactus has a strong root system that can support about 9–10 tons (8–9 t) of growth. Its spines can measure up to 2.5 inches (5 cm) long. Saguaro cacti live for about 170 years. The giant cacti can be found from southeastern California to southern Arizona.

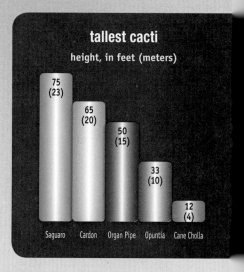

tallest cacti

height, in feet (meters)

Saguaro	Cardon	Organ Pipe	Opuntia	Cane Cholla
75 (23)	65 (20)	50 (15)	33 (10)	12 (4)

tallest tree

California Redwood

Growing in both California and southern Oregon, California redwoods can reach a height of 385 feet (117 m). Their trunks can grow up to 25 feet (8 m) in diameter. The tallest redwood on record is more than 60 feet (18 m) taller than the Statue of Liberty. Amazingly, this giant tree grows from a seed the size of a tomato. Some redwoods are believed to be more than 2,000 years old. The trees' thick bark and foliage protect them from natural hazards, such as insects and fires.

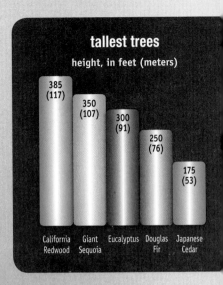

tallest trees
height, in feet (meters)

California Redwood	Giant Sequoia	Eucalyptus	Douglas Fir	Japanese Cedar
385 (117)	350 (107)	300 (91)	250 (76)	175 (53)

most poisonous mushroom

Death Cap

Death cap mushrooms are members of the Amanita family, which are among the most dangerous mushrooms in the world. The death cap contains deadly peptide toxins that cause rapid loss of bodily fluids and intense thirst. Within six hours, the poison shuts down the kidneys, liver, and central nervous system, causing coma and—in more than 50 percent of cases—death. Estimates of the number of poisonous mushroom species range from 80 to 2,000. Most experts agree, however, that at least 100 varieties will cause severe symptoms and even death if eaten.

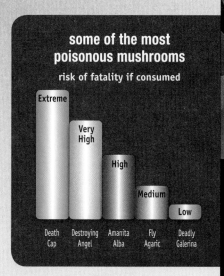

some of the most poisonous mushrooms
risk of fatality if consumed

Death Cap	Destroying Angel	Amanita Alba	Fly Agaric	Deadly Galerina
Extreme	Very High	High	Medium	Low

largest flower

Rafflesia

The blossoms of the giant rafflesia—or stinking corpse lily—can reach 36 inches (91 cm) in diameter and weigh up to 25 pounds (11 kg). Its petals can grow 1.5 feet (0.5 m) long and 1 inch (2.5 cm) thick. There are 16 different species of rafflesia. This endangered plant is found only in the rain forests of Borneo and Sumatra. It lives inside the bark of host vines and is noticeable only when its flowers break through to blossom. The large, reddish purple flowers give off a smell similar to rotting meat, which attracts insects that help spread the rafflesia's pollen.

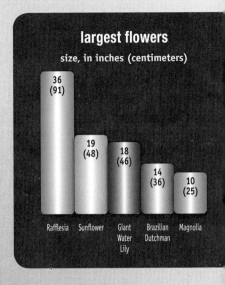

largest flowers

size, in inches (centimeters)

Rafflesia	Sunflower	Giant Water Lily	Brazilian Dutchman	Magnolia
36 (91)	19 (48)	18 (46)	14 (36)	10 (25)

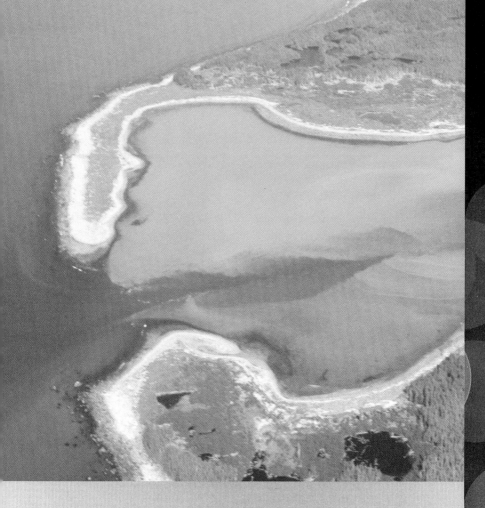

highest tsunami wave since 1900

Lituya Bay

A 1,720-foot (524 m) tsunami wave crashed down in Lituya Bay, Alaska, on July 9, 1958. Located in Glacier Bay National Park, the tsunami was caused by a massive landslide that was triggered by an 8.3-magnitude earthquake. The water from the bay covered 5 square miles (13 sq km) of land and traveled inland as far as 3,600 feet (1,097 m). Millions of trees were washed away. Amazingly, because the area was very isolated and the coastline was sheltered by coves, only two people died when their fishing boat sank.

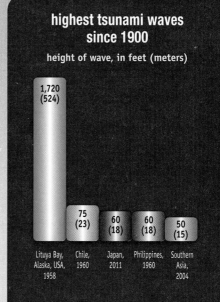

highest tsunami waves since 1900

height of wave, in feet (meters)

Lituya Bay, Alaska, USA, 1958	Chile, 1960	Japan, 2011	Philippines, 1960	Southern Asia, 2004
1,720 (524)	75 (23)	60 (18)	60 (18)	50 (15)

179

most intense earthquake since 1900

Chile

An explosive earthquake measuring 9.5 on the Richter scale rocked the coast of Chile on May 22, 1960. This is equal to the intensity of about 60,000 hydrogen bombs. Some 2,000 people were killed and another 3,000 injured. The death toll was fairly low because the foreshocks frightened people into the streets. When the massive jolt came, many of the buildings that collapsed were already empty. The coastal towns of Valdivia and Puerto Montt suffered the most damage because they were closest to the epicenter—located about 100 miles (161 km) offshore. On February 27, 2010, Chile was rocked by another huge earthquake (8.8 magnitude), but the loss of life and property was much less than from previous quakes.

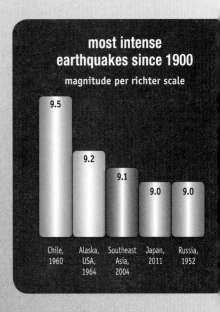

most intense earthquakes since 1900

magnitude per richter scale

Chile, 1960	Alaska, USA, 1964	Southeast Asia, 2004	Japan, 2011	Russia, 1952
9.5	9.2	9.1	9.0	9.0

most destructive flood since 1900

Hurricane Katrina

The pounding rain and storm surges of Hurricane Katrina resulted in catastrophic flooding that cost about $60 billion. The storm formed in late August 2005 over the Bahamas, moved across Florida, and finally hit Louisiana on August 29 as a category-3 storm. The storm surge from the Gulf of Mexico flooded the state, as well as neighboring Alabama and Mississippi. Many levees could not hold back the massive amounts of water, and entire towns were destroyed. In total, some 1,800 people lost their lives.

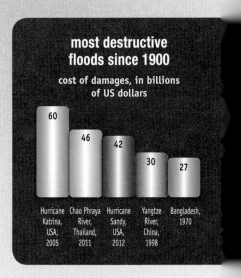

most destructive floods since 1900

cost of damages, in billions of US dollars

60	46	42	30	27
Hurricane Katrina, USA, 2005	Chao Phraya River, Thailand, 2011	Hurricane Sandy, USA, 2012	Yangtze River, China, 1998	Bangladesh, 1970

worst oil spill

Gulf War

During the Gulf War in 1991, Iraqi troops opened valves of oil wells in Kuwait, releasing more than 240 million gallons (908 million L) of oil into the Persian Gulf. At its worst, the spill measured 101 miles by 42 miles (163 km by 68 km) and was about 5 inches (13 cm) thick. Some of the oil eventually evaporated, another 1 million barrels were collected out of the water, and the rest washed ashore. Although much of the oil can no longer be seen, most of it remains, soaked into the deeper layers of sand along the coast. Amazingly, the wildlife that lives in these areas were not harmed as much as was initially feared. However, salt marsh areas without strong currents were hit the hardest, as oil collected there and killed off entire ecosystems.

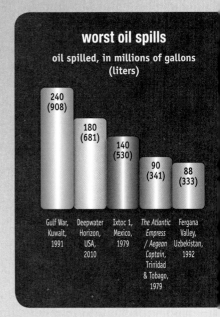

worst oil spills

oil spilled, in millions of gallons (liters)

240 (908)	180 (681)	140 (530)	90 (341)	88 (333)
Gulf War, Kuwait, 1991	Deepwater Horizon, USA, 2010	Ixtoc 1, Mexico, 1979	The Atlantic Empress / Aegean Captain, Trinidad & Tobago, 1979	Fergana Valley, Uzbekistan, 1992

most destructive tornado since 1900

Joplin, Missouri

On May 22, 2011, a category EF5 tornado ripped through Joplin, Missouri, and destroyed about 2,000 buildings, or 25 percent, of the small Midwest town. The devastating storm caused damage totaling $2.8 billion and killed 161 people. The tornado measured up to a mile (1.6 km) wide, and was part of a large outbreak of storms during that week, which affected Arkansas, Kansas, and Oklahoma. A category-5 tornado on the Enhanced Fujita (EF) scale is the most intense, capable of producing winds greater than 200 miles (322 km) per hour. With more than 1,000 storms popping up across the country, 2011 was the deadliest year for tornadoes in fifty years.

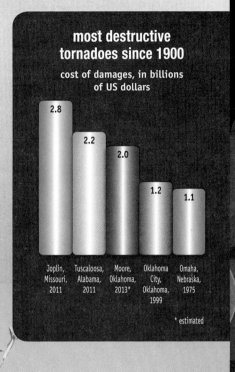

most destructive tornadoes since 1900

cost of damages, in billions of US dollars

Joplin, Missouri, 2011	Tuscaloosa, Alabama, 2011	Moore, Oklahoma, 2013*	Oklahoma City, Oklahoma, 1999	Omaha, Nebraska, 1975
2.8	2.2	2.0	1.2	1.1

* estimated

Devastation from Hurricane Camille

most intense hurricanes since 1900

Hurricane Allen & Hurricane Camille

Both Hurricane Allen and Hurricane Camille were category 5 storms with winds that gusted up to 190 miles (306 km) per hour. Hurricane Camille made landfall in the United States along the mouth of the Mississippi River on August 17, 1969. The Gulf Coast and Virginia sustained the most damage, and the total storm damages cost $1.42 billion. Hurricane Allen sustained its strongest winds near Puerto Rico on August 5, 1980. The storm traveled through the Caribbean, Cuba, the Yucatan Peninsula, and the south-central United States. The damages totaled about $1 billion.

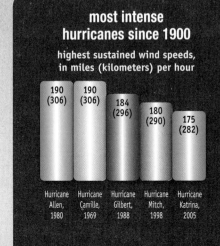

most intense hurricanes since 1900

highest sustained wind speeds, in miles (kilometers) per hour

190 (306)	190 (306)	184 (296)	180 (290)	175 (282)
Hurricane Allen, 1980	Hurricane Camille, 1969	Hurricane Gilbert, 1988	Hurricane Mitch, 1998	Hurricane Katrina, 2005

greenest company in the united states

IBM

Information and service provider IBM received a green score of 82.9 from media giant *Newsweek*. To determine this ranking, *Newsweek* arrived at these scores by researching the ways that companies conduct their business in environmentally friendly ways, such as recycling material, protecting resources, and saving electricity. For the second straight year, IBM grabbed the top spot with its green product line called Smarter Planet. These products help other companies determine which items they truly need to do business, while eliminating the extra waste and saving money and resources.

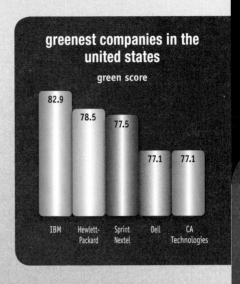

greenest companies in the united states

green score

Company	Score
IBM	82.9
Hewlett-Packard	78.5
Sprint Nextel	77.5
Dell	77.1
CA Technologies	77.1

START
GREEN RESPONSIBILITY

MEETING POINT   MEETING POINT

Smack in the Middle

Belle Fourche, South Dakota, is the geographic center of the United States. When Alaska and Hawaii were added to the Union in 1959, it put this small rural town right in the middle of the country. About 20 miles (32.1 km) north of town, there is a 21-foot (6.4-m) wide monument in the shape of a compass made from South Dakota granite.

Not a Lot of Ground to Cover

There's only one place in the United States where four states touch—Four Corners Monument. Here, the corners of Arizona, Colorado, New Mexico, and Utah come together under a granite-and-brass monument. So, in just a few steps, visitors can pass through four states in less than 30 seconds.

Meet Me on Main Street

There are about 10,466 Main Streets located throughout the United States. One of the longest Main Streets is located in Island Park, Idaho, and stretches for 33 miles (53.1 km). The town, which has a very narrow but very long shape, hugs the street. Only about 300 people live there.

Keep On Truckin'

There are about 4 million miles (6.4 million km) of highways, roads, and streets in the United States—that's enough to circle Earth more than 160 times. There are also 600,000 bridges that span these thoroughfares. Each year, drivers cover about 2.94 billion miles (4.73 km) across the country.

Scout's Honor

The Girl Scouts have 2.3 million girls in their program, while there are 2.7 million boys involved in Tiger, Cub, and Boy Scouts. The girls sell more than $750 million in cookies each year to support their troops. Boys earn more than 2 million merit badges, with first aid, swimming, and environmental science being most popular.

Helping Hands

Americans love to help each other out. About 64.5 million people—or 26.5 percent of the country—lend their time to at least one organization throughout the year. The average volunteer donates about 50 hours of his or her time annually. The most popular types of organizations to volunteer for are religious (33.1 percent), educational or youth service (25.5 percent), and social or community service (14.2 percent).

Free-time Fillers

The most popular hobby among Americans is watching television, with more than half of all leisure time spent in front of the tube. Online gaming is also extremely popular, with young people racking up 10,000 hours by the time they turn 21. Americans also like vacations—they take about 1.5 billion leisure trips a year. And three out of every four Americans go to the movies at least once annually.

state with the oldest mardi gras celebration

Alabama

People in Mobile, Alabama, have been celebrating Mardi Gras since 1703, although they did not have an official parade event until 1831. After a brief hiatus during the Civil War, the celebrations started back up in 1866 and have been growing ever since. Today, some 100,000 people gather in Mobile to enjoy the 40 parades that take place during the two weeks that lead up to Mardi Gras. On the biggest day—Fat Tuesday— six parades wind through the downtown waterfront, with floats and costumed dancers. But at the stroke of midnight, the partying stops and plans for the next year begin.

united states' oldest mardi gras celebrations

number of years since celebration began

Mobile, Alabama (1831)	New Orleans, Louisiana (1835)	Lafayette, Louisiana (1842)	Pensacola, Florida (1844)	Galveston, Texas (1867)
182	178	171	169	146

*As of 2013

state with the largest national forest

Alaska

The Tongass National Forest covers approximately 16,800,000 acres (6,798,900 ha) in southeast Alaska. That's about the same size as West Virginia. It is also home to the world's largest temperate rain forest. Some of the forest's trees are more than 700 years old. About 11,000 miles (17,703 km) of shoreline are inside the park. Some of the animals that live in the forest include bears, salmon, and wolves. The world's largest group of bald eagles also spend the fall and winter here on the Chilkat River.

united states' largest national forests

size, in millions of acres (hectares)

Forest	Size
Tongass National Forest, Alaska	16.8 (6.8)
Humboldt-Toiyabe National Forest, California/Nevada	6.3 (1.5)
Chugach National Forest, Alaska	5.4 (2.1)
Tonto National Forest, Arizona	2.8 (1.1)
Boise National Forest, Idaho	2.6 (1.1)

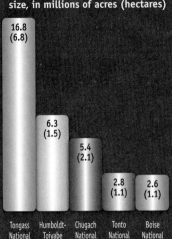

state with the largest collection of telescopes

Arizona

The Kitt Peak National Observatory is home to 24 different telescopes—22 optical telescopes and 2 radio telescopes. Located above the Sonora Desert, the site was chosen to house the collection of equipment because of its clear weather, low relative humidity, and steady atmosphere. Eight different astronomical research institutions maintain and operate the telescopes. The observatory is overseen by the National Optical Astronomy Observatories. One of the most prominent telescopes at Kitt Peak is the McMath-Pierce Solar Telescope, the second-largest solar telescope in the world.

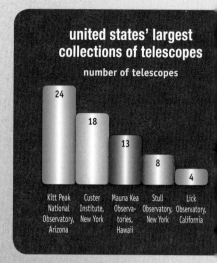

united states' largest collections of telescopes
number of telescopes

Kitt Peak National Observatory, Arizona	Custer Institute, New York	Mauna Kea Observatories, Hawaii	Stull Observatory, New York	Lick Observatory, California
24	18	13	8	4

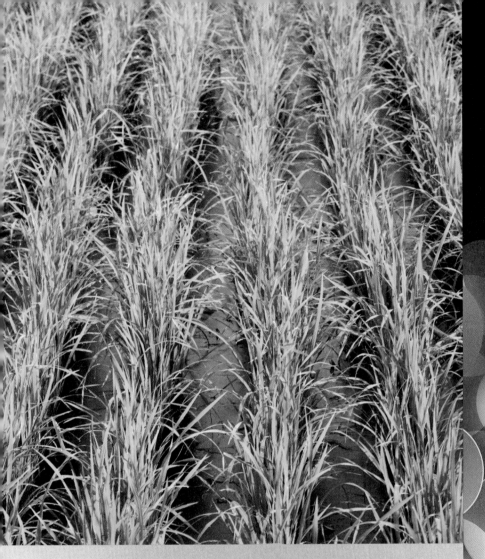

state that grows the most rice

Arkansas

Farmers in Arkansas produced 4.79 million tons (4.3 million t) of rice in 2012, which was more than 48 percent of all rice grown in the country. With that harvest, farmers could give every person in the United States 30 pounds (13 kg) of rice and still have a little left over. There are more than 1.19 million acres (484,004 ha) of rice planted across Arkansas. Agriculture is a very important part of the state's economy, employing more than 287,000 workers, or about 20 percent of the state's workforce.

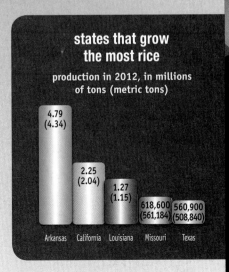

states that grow the most rice

production in 2012, in millions of tons (metric tons)

Arkansas	California	Louisiana	Missouri	Texas
4.79 (4.34)	2.25 (2.04)	1.27 (1.15)	618,600 (561,184)	560,900 (508,840)

state with the most-visited zoo

California

The San Diego Zoo draws about 3.4 million visitors each year. The zoo is located in Balboa Park, California, and showcases more than 3,700 animals, including mammals, reptiles, birds, and insects. Visitors can explore the 100-acre (40.4 ha) zoo by tour bus or the Skyfari—a gondola ride above the park. Some of the most popular exhibits include the Panda Canyon, Africa Rocks, Urban Jungle, Outback, Northern Frontier, and Elephant Odyssey. The zoo also offers special education programs and behind-the-scenes tours to help visitors learn more about the animal residents.

194

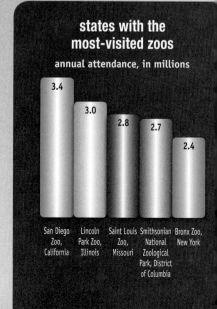

states with the most-visited zoos

annual attendance, in millions

3.4	3.0	2.8	2.7	2.4
San Diego Zoo, California	Lincoln Park Zoo, Illinois	Saint Louis Zoo, Missouri	Smithsonian National Zoological Park, District of Columbia	Bronx Zoo, New York

state with the tallest sand dunes

Colorado

Star Dune, located in Great Sand Dunes National Park near Mosca, Colorado, is 750 feet (229 m) tall. That's almost five times taller than the Statue of Liberty! The park's dunes were formed from sand left behind by evaporated lakes. Wind picked up the sand and funneled it through the surrounding mountains until it collected in this low-lying region. Visitors to the park are allowed to ski, sled, or slide down the giant dunes; this works best after a light rain. Many animals also call this park home, including pika, marmots, black bears, and mountain lions.

united states' tallest sand dunes
height, in feet (meters)

Great Sand Dunes, Colorado	Eureka Dunes, California	Kelso Dunes, California	Sand Mountain, Nevada	Oregon Dunes, California
750 (229)	682 (208)	600 (183)	600 (183)	500 (152)

state with the oldest amusement park

Connecticut

Lake Compounce in Bristol, Connecticut, first opened as a picnic park in 1846. The park's first electric roller coaster, the Green Dragon, was introduced in 1914 and cost ten cents per ride. It was replaced by the Wildcat in 1927, and the wooden coaster still operates today. In 1996 the park got a $50 million upgrade, which included the thrilling new roller coaster Boulder Dash. It is the only coaster to be built into a mountainside. Another $3.3 million was spent on upgrades in 2005, including an 800-foot (244 m) lazy river.

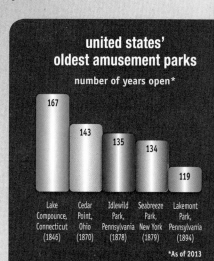

united states'
oldest amusement parks
number of years open*

Lake Compounce, Connecticut (1846)	Cedar Point, Ohio (1870)	Idlewild Park, Pennsylvania (1878)	Seabreeze Park, New York (1879)	Lakemont Park, Pennsylvania (1894)
167	143	135	134	119

*As of 2013

state with the largest pumpkin-throwing contest

Delaware

Each year approximately 20,000 people gather in Sussex County, Delaware, for the annual World Championship Punkin Chunkin. More than 70 teams compete during the three-day festival to see who can chuck their pumpkin the farthest. Each team constructs a machine that has a mechanical or compressed-air firing device—no explosives are allowed. The farthest a pumpkin has traveled during the championship is 4,483.5 feet (1,366 m), or the length of twelve football fields. Although the 2012 competition was delayed a day by Superstorm Sandy, more than 70 teams competed during the event. The first Punkin Chunkin competition was held in 1986.

united states' largest pumpkin-throwing contests

number of spectators

Bridgeville, Delaware	Amherst, Massachusetts	Morton, Illinois	Moab, Utah	Stowe, Vermont
20,000	4,500	4,000	2,000	1,500

197

state with the most lightning strikes

Florida

Southern Florida is known as the Lightning Capital of the United States, with 25.3 bolts occurring over each square mile (2.6 sq km)—the equivalent of ten city blocks—each year. Some 70 percent of all strikes occur between noon and 6:00 p.m., and the most dangerous months are July and August. Most lightning bolts measure 2 to 3 miles (5.2 to 7.8 km) long and can generate between 100 million and 1 billion volts of electricity. The air in a lightning bolt is heated to 50,000°F (27,760°C).

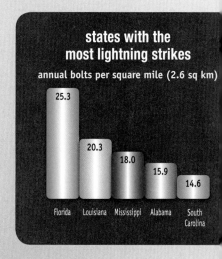

states with the most lightning strikes
annual bolts per square mile (2.6 sq km)

Florida	Louisiana	Mississippi	Alabama	South Carolina
25.3	20.3	18.0	15.9	14.6

state with the largest sports hall of fame

Georgia

The Georgia Sports Hall of Fame fills 43,000 square feet (3,995 sq m) with memorabilia from Georgia's most accomplished college, amateur, and professional athletes. Some 230,000 bricks, 245 tons (222 t) of steel, and 7,591 pounds (3,443 kg) of glass were used in its construction. The hall owns more than 3,000 artifacts and displays about 1,000 of them at a time. Some Hall of Famers include baseball legend Hank Aaron, Olympic basketball great Theresa Edwards, and Super Bowl I champion Bill Curry.

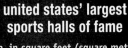

united states' largest sports halls of fame

area, in square feet (square meters)

Georgia Sports Hall of Fame	Virginia Sports Hall of Fame	Texas Sports Hall of Fame	Alabama Sports Hall of Fame	Mississippi Sports Hall of Fame
43,000 (3,995)	35,000 (3,252)	35,000 (3,252)	33,000 (3,066)	21,542 (2,001)

199

state with the world's largest submillimeter wavelength telescope

Hawaii

Mauna Kea—located on the island of Hawaii—is home to the world's largest submillimeter wavelength telescope, with a diameter of 49 feet (15 m). The James Clerk Maxwell Telescope (JCMT) is used to study our solar system, interstellar dust and gas, and distant galaxies. Mauna Kea also houses one of the world's largest optical/infrared (Keck I and II) and dedicated infrared (UKIRT) telescopes in the world. Mauna Kea is an ideal spot for astronomy because the atmosphere above the dormant volcano is very dry with little cloud cover, and its distance from city lights ensures a clear night sky.

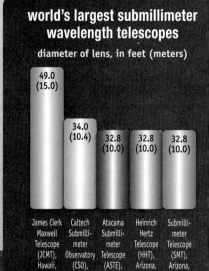

world's largest submillimeter wavelength telescopes

diameter of lens, in feet (meters)

James Clerk Maxwell Telescope (JCMT), Hawaii, USA	Caltech Submillimeter Observatory (CSO), Hawaii, USA	Atacama Submillimeter Telescope (ASTE), Chile	Heinrich Hertz Telescope (HHT), Arizona, USA	Submillimeter Telescope (SMT), Arizona, USA
49.0 (15.0)	34.0 (10.4)	32.8 (10.0)	32.8 (10.0)	32.8 (10.0)

state that harvests the most farm-raised trout

Idaho

Idaho topped farm-raised trout sales in 2012 with a total of $43.6 million—about 55 percent of the total trout sales in the United States. Trout farmers in the state sold about 30.9 million fish with a combined weight of 36.6 million pounds (16.6 million k). That's enough fish to feed everyone in the state a meal per week for a year. There are about 115 aquaculture facilities in the state. About 98 percent of aquaculture production takes place along the Snake River in Gooding, Twin Falls, and Jerome counties. Fish hatcheries first opened in Idaho in the 1930s.

states that harvest the most farm-raised trout

sales in 2012, in millions of US dollars

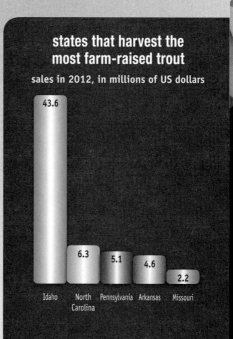

Idaho	North Carolina	Pennsylvania	Arkansas	Missouri
43.6	6.3	5.1	4.6	2.2

state with the largest public college library

Illinois

The library at the University of Illinois at Urbana-Champaign has more than 10.5 million books on its shelves. The student body is made up of approximately 32,200 undergraduates and 12,200 graduate students. If each of these students checked out 235 books, there would still be some left in the library. The most popular majors at the school include finance, engineering, and social sciences. The University of Illinois at Urbana-Champaign is situated on a 1,783-acre (721.5 ha) campus, and is located about 130 miles (209.2 km) south of Chicago.

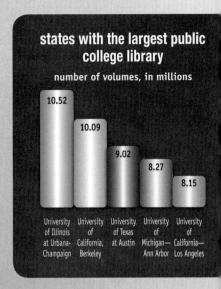

states with the largest public college library

number of volumes, in millions

University of Illinois at Urbana-Champaign	University of California, Berkeley	University of Texas at Austin	University of Michigan—Ann Arbor	University of California—Los Angeles
10.52	10.09	9.02	8.27	8.15

state with the largest half marathon

Indiana

Cars aren't the only things racing in Indianapolis, Indiana. Each May some 35,000 runners take part in the OneAmerica 500 Festival Mini-Marathon. This makes the Mini-Marathon the nation's largest half marathon and the nation's eighth-longest road race. The 13.1-mile (21.1 km) race winds through downtown and includes a lap along the Indianapolis Motor Speedway oval. A giant pasta dinner and after-race party await the runners at the end of the day. The Mini-Marathon is part of a weekend celebration that centers around the Indianapolis 500 auto race.

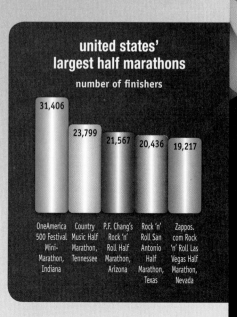

united states' largest half marathons

number of finishers

31,406	23,799	21,567	20,436	19,217
OneAmerica 500 Festival Mini-Marathon, Indiana	Country Music Half Marathon, Tennessee	P.F. Chang's Rock 'n' Roll Half Marathon, Arizona	Rock 'n' Roll San Antonio Half Marathon, Texas	Zappos. com Rock 'n' Roll Las Vegas Half Marathon, Nevada

state with the highest egg production

Iowa

Iowa tops all other states in the country in egg production, turning out almost 14.5 billion eggs per year. That's enough to give every person in the United States about three and a half dozen eggs each! That's a good thing, because each person in America eats about 248 eggs per year. The state has 57 million laying hens, and each is capable of laying about 254 eggs a year. These hungry hens eat about 57 million bushels of corn and 28.5 million bushels of soybeans annually. In addition to selling the eggs as they are, Iowa's processing plants turn them into frozen, liquid, dried, or specialty egg products.

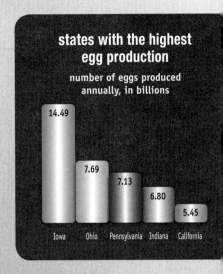

states with the highest egg production

number of eggs produced annually, in billions

Iowa	Ohio	Pennsylvania	Indiana	California
14.49	7.69	7.13	6.80	5.45

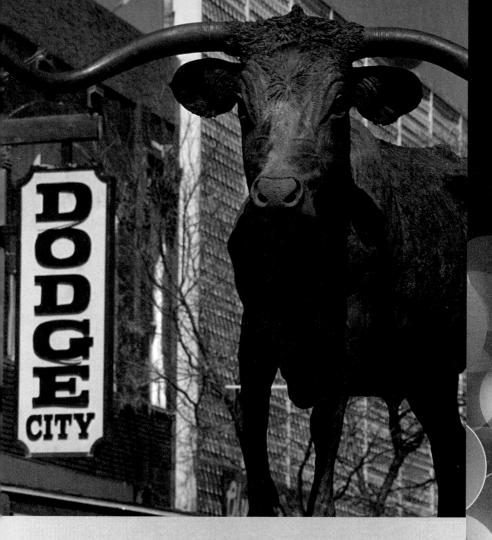

state with the windiest city

Kansas

According to average annual wind speeds collected by the National Climatic Data Center, Dodge City, Kansas, is the windiest city in the United States, with an average wind speed of 13.9 miles (22.3 km) per hour. Located in Ford County, the city borders the Santa Fe Trail and is rich in history. The city was founded in 1872 and had a reputation as a tough cowboy town. With help from legendary sheriffs like Wyatt Earp, order was established and the town grew steadily. Today, tourists come to learn about the area's history.

united states' windiest cities

average wind speed, in miles (kilometers) per hour

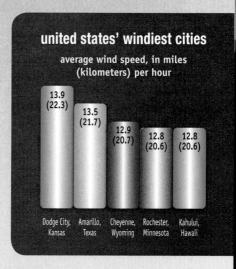

Dodge City, Kansas	Amarillo, Texas	Cheyenne, Wyoming	Rochester, Minnesota	Kahului, Hawaii
13.9 (22.3)	13.5 (21.7)	12.9 (20.7)	12.8 (20.6)	12.8 (20.6)

205

state with the most popular horse race

Kentucky

Each year, the Kentucky Derby draws more than 165,000 people who gather to watch "the most exciting two minutes in sports." The race is run at Churchill Downs in Louisville, on a dirt track that measures 1.25 miles (2 km) long. The thoroughbred horses must be three years old to race, and the winner nabs a $2 million purse. The winning horse is covered in a blanket of 554 red roses, which gave the race the nickname "The Run for the Roses." The fastest horse to complete the race was Secretariat in 1973, with a time of 1:59:40.

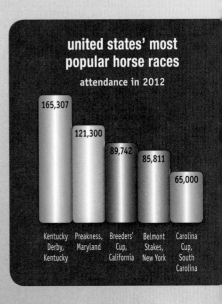

united states' most popular horse races

attendance in 2012

Kentucky Derby, Kentucky	Preakness, Maryland	Breeders' Cup, California	Belmont Stakes, New York	Carolina Cup, South Carolina
165,307	121,300	89,742	85,811	65,000

Secretariat

state with the tallest capitol building

Louisiana

The Louisiana State Capitol rises 460 feet (140.2 m) above Baton Rouge. The 34-story building is the tallest in the city, and the seventh-tallest building in the state. It is home to the Louisiana State Legislature, and the governor and lieutenant governor's offices. Opened to the public in May 1932, the Louisiana State Capitol took 29 months to complete and cost $5 million. The art deco building's main tower includes sculptures that depict important events in Louisiana's history. The Capitol Gardens are on the surrounding 30 acres (12 ha), and 10 miles (16.1 km) of sidewalks wind through the grounds. The building is a National Historic Landmark.

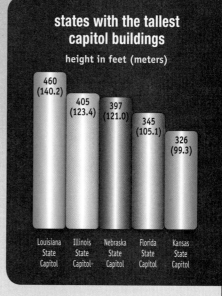

states with the tallest capitol buildings
height in feet (meters)

Louisiana State Capitol	Illinois State Capitol	Nebraska State Capitol	Florida State Capitol	Kansas State Capitol
460 (140.2)	405 (123.4)	397 (121.0)	345 (105.1)	326 (99.3)

207

state with the oldest state fair

Maine

The first Skowhegan State Fair took place in 1819—a year before Maine officially became a state! The fair took place in January, and hundreds of people came despite harsh weather. Originally sponsored by the Somerset Central Agricultural Society, the fair name became official in 1842. State fairs were very important in the 1800s. With no agricultural colleges in existence, fairs became the best way for farmers to learn about new agricultural methods and equipment. Today, the Skowhegan State Fair features more than 7,000 exhibitors who compete for prize money totaling more than $200,000. The fair also includes a demolition derby, a children's barnyard, concerts, livestock exhibits, and arts and crafts.

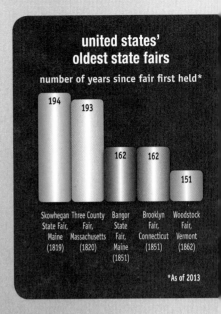

united states' oldest state fairs

number of years since fair first held*

194	193	162	162	151
Skowhegan State Fair, Maine (1819)	Three County Fair, Massachusetts (1820)	Bangor State Fair, Maine (1851)	Brooklyn Fair, Connecticut (1851)	Woodstock Fair, Vermont (1862)

*As of 2013

College Park Aviation Museum

state with the oldest airport

Maryland

The Wright brothers founded College Park Airport in 1909 to teach army officers how to fly, and it has been in operation ever since. The airport is now owned by the Maryland-National Capital Park and Planning Commission and is on the Register of Historic Places. Many aviation "firsts" occurred at this airport, such as the first woman passenger in the United States (1909), the first test of a bomb-dropping device (1911), and the first US airmail service (1918). The College Park Aviation Museum is located on its grounds, and it exhibits aviation memorabilia.

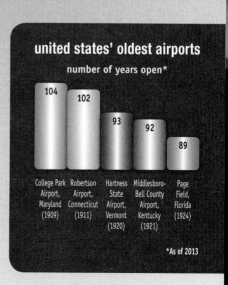

united states' oldest airports
number of years open*

College Park Airport, Maryland (1909)	Robertson Airport, Connecticut (1911)	Hartness State Airport, Vermont (1920)	Middlesboro-Bell County Airport, Kentucky (1921)	Page Field, Florida (1924)
104	102	93	92	89

*As of 2013

209

state with the oldest baseball stadium

Massachusetts

Fenway Park opened its doors to Massachusetts baseball fans on April 20, 1912. The Boston Red Sox—the park's home team—won the World Series that year. The park celebrated in 2004 when the Sox won the World Series again. The park is also the home of the Green Monster—a giant 37-foot (11.3 m) wall with an additional 23-foot (7 m) screen that has plagued home-run hitters since the park first opened. The park's unique dimensions were not intended to prevent home runs, however; they were meant to keep nonpaying fans outside. A seat out in the right-field bleachers is painted red to mark where the longest measurable home run hit inside the park landed. It measured 502 feet (153 m) and was hit by Ted Williams in 1946. Some of the other baseball legends who played at Fenway include Cy Young, Babe Ruth, Jimmie Fox, and Carlton Fisk.

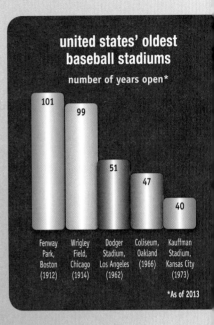

united states' oldest baseball stadiums

number of years open*

Fenway Park, Boston (1912)	Wrigley Field, Chicago (1914)	Dodger Stadium, Los Angeles (1962)	Coliseum, Oakland (1966)	Kauffman Stadium, Kansas City (1973)
101	99	51	47	40

*As of 2013

BOSTON RED SOX

state with the largest stadium

Michigan

Michigan Stadium—also known as the Big House—is the home of the University of Michigan Wolverines, and can hold 109,901 football fans during the home games. The stadium was constructed in 1927 using 440 tons (399 t) of reinforcing steel and 31,000 square feet (2,880 sq m) of wire mesh to create an 82,000-seat venue. After several renovations, the stadium reached its current seating capacity in 2010. The most recent additions include luxury boxes and club seating. Since its inaugural game, Michigan Stadium has hosted more than 35 million fans.

united states' largest stadiums

seating capacity

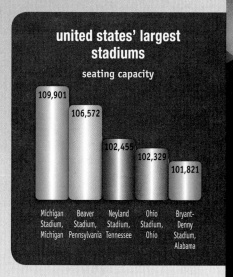

Michigan Stadium, Michigan	Beaver Stadium, Pennsylvania	Neyland Stadium, Tennessee	Ohio Stadium, Ohio	Bryant-Denny Stadium, Alabama
109,901	106,572	102,455	102,329	101,821

state with the largest indoor amusement park

Minnesota

Nickelodeon Universe is located inside the Mall of America in Bloomington, Minnesota, and covers 7 acres (2.8 ha). The park offers more than 20 rides, including the SpongeBob SquarePants Rock Bottom Plunge, Splat-O-Sphere, Teenage Mutant Ninja Turtles Shell Shock, Log Chute, the Fairly Odd Coaster, and Avatar Airbender. Some of the other attractions at the park are a rock-climbing wall, petting zoo, and game arcade. Kids can also meet Dora, Diego, Blue, and SpongeBob.

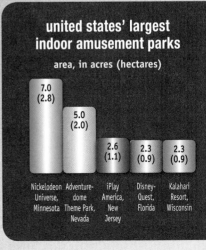

united states' largest indoor amusement parks

area, in acres (hectares)

Nickelodeon Universe, Minnesota	Adventure-dome Theme Park, Nevada	iPlay America, New Jersey	Disney-Quest, Florida	Kalahari Resort, Wisconsin
7.0 (2.8)	5.0 (2.0)	2.6 (1.1)	2.3 (0.9)	2.3 (0.9)

state with the most catfish

Mississippi

Mississippi sold $175 million in catfish in 2012. There are about 388 million catfish in Mississippi—more than 60 percent of the world's farm-raised supply. That's almost enough to give every person in the state about 132 fish each. There are about 80,200 water acres (32,000 ha) used to farm catfish in Mississippi. The state's residents are quite proud of their successful fish industry and celebrate at the World Catfish Festival in Belzoni.

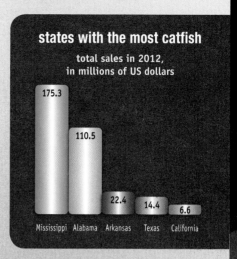

states with the most catfish
total sales in 2012,
in millions of US dollars

Mississippi	Alabama	Arkansas	Texas	California
175.3	110.5	22.4	14.4	6.6

state with the largest outdoor theater

Missouri

The Municipal Theatre in St. Louis, Missouri—affectionately known as the Muny—is the nation's largest outdoor theater, with 80,000 square feet (7,432 sq m) and 11,500 seats—about the same size as a regulation soccer field. Amazingly, construction for the giant theater was completed in just 42 days at a cost of $10,000. The theater opened in 1917 with a production of Verdi's *Aïda*, and the best seats cost only $1. The Muny offers classic Broadway shows each summer, with past productions including *The King and I*, *The Wizard of Oz*, and *Oliver!* The last nine rows of the theater are always held as free seats for the public, just as they have been since the Muny opened.

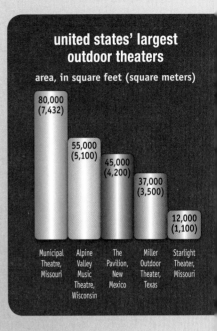

united states' largest outdoor theaters

area, in square feet (square meters)

Municipal Theatre, Missouri	Alpine Valley Music Theatre, Wisconsin	The Pavilion, New Mexico	Miller Outdoor Theater, Texas	Starlight Theater, Missouri
80,000 (7,432)	55,000 (5,100)	45,000 (4,200)	37,000 (3,500)	12,000 (1,100)

state with the largest concrete statue

Montana

Our Lady of the Rockies is an 88.6-foot (27 m) concrete sculpture of a woman in a flowing dress that stands on top of the Continental Divide overlooking Butte, Montana. It was completed in 1985, and is dedicated to all women, especially mothers. The statue stands 8,510 feet (2,593 m) above sea level. Its head is 16 feet (4.8 m) high by 10 feet (3 m) wide and features a 4-foot-long (1.2 m) nose. The width of the statue—from fingertip to fingertip—measures 48 feet (14.6 m). Our Lady of the Rockies weighs 51 tons (46.2 t). The project began in 1979 and took six years to complete.

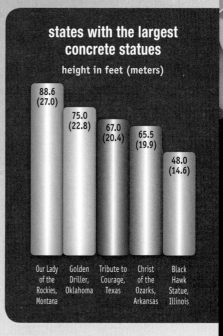

states with the largest concrete statues

height in feet (meters)

Our Lady of the Rockies, Montana	Golden Driller, Oklahoma	Tribute to Courage, Texas	Christ of the Ozarks, Arkansas	Black Hawk Statue, Illinois
88.6 (27.0)	75.0 (22.8)	67.0 (20.4)	65.5 (19.9)	48.0 (14.6)

state with the world's largest indoor rain forest

Nebraska

At 123,000 square feet (11,427 sq m), the Lied Jungle at the Henry Doorly Zoo in Omaha is the world's largest indoor rain forest. The eight-story-tall building houses rain-forest exhibits from Asia, Africa, and South America that include plants, trees, caves, cliffs, bridges, and waterfalls. Some ninety different animals species live in these exhibits, including gibbons, small-clawed otters, spider monkeys, pygmy hippos, tapirs, and many birds and reptiles. Some exotic tree species include chocolate, allspice, African sausage, and black pepper. The giant roof lets in sunlight to promote natural growth. The jungle opened in 1992 and cost $15 million to create.

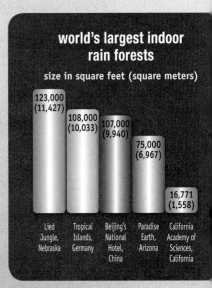

world's largest indoor rain forests

size in square feet (square meters)

123,000 (11,427)	108,000 (10,033)	107,000 (9,940)	75,000 (6,967)	16,771 (1,558)
Lied Jungle, Nebraska	Tropical Islands, Germany	Beijing's National Hotel, China	Paradise Earth, Arizona	California Academy of Sciences, California

state with the largest glass sculpture

Nevada

Fiori di Como—the breathtaking chandelier at the Bellagio Hotel in Las Vegas, Nevada—measures 65.7 feet by 29.5 feet (20 m by 9 m). Created by Dale Chihuly, the handblown glass chandelier consists of more than 2,000 discs of colored glass. Each disc is about 18 inches (45.7 cm) wide and hangs about 20 feet (6.1 m) overhead. Together, these colorful discs look like a giant field of flowers. The chandelier required about 10,000 pounds (4,536 kg) of steel and 40,000 pounds (18,144 kg) of handblown glass. The sculpture's name translates to "Flowers of Como." The Bellagio was modeled after a hotel on Lake Como in Italy.

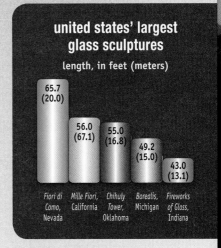

united states' largest glass sculptures

length, in feet (meters)

65.7 (20.0)	56.0 (67.1)	55.0 (16.8)	49.2 (15.0)	43.0 (13.1)
Fiori di Como, Nevada	Mille Fiori, California	Chihuly Tower, Oklahoma	Borealis, Michigan	Fireworks of Glass, Indiana

state with the oldest lottery

New Hampshire

New Hampshire was the first state to establish a legal lottery system when it sold its first ticket in 1964. The lottery was originally created to raise money for charitable causes throughout the state. Since it began, the New Hampshire Lottery has seen more than $4.1 billion in sales and other earnings—about $2.7 billion was paid out as prize money, and about $1.3 billion has gone to fund education in the state. The main in-state lottery in New Hampshire is called the Weekly Grand, but residents participate in several multistate lotteries as well.

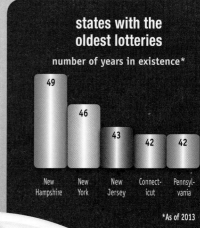

states with the oldest lotteries

number of years in existence*

New Hampshire	New York	New Jersey	Connecticut	Pennsylvania
49	46	43	42	42

*As of 2013

state with the world's longest boardwalk

New Jersey

The famous boardwalk in Atlantic City, New Jersey, stretches for 4 miles (6.4 km) along the beach. Combined with the adjoining boardwalk in Ventnor, the length increases to just under 6 miles (9.7 km). The 60-foot (18 m) wide boardwalk opened on June 26, 1870. It was the first boardwalk built in the United States, and was designed to keep sand out of the tourists' shoes. Today, the boardwalk is filled with amusement parks, shops, restaurants, and hotels. Some sections of the boardwalk were damaged during Superstorm Sandy in October 2012. However, recovery efforts have restored much of the boardwalk to its original state. Those sections that have not already been repaired are expected to be completed by the 2014 summer season.

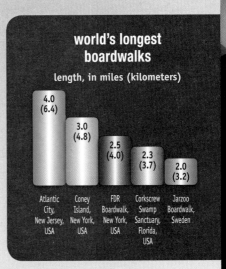

world's longest boardwalks

length, in miles (kilometers)

Location	Length
Atlantic City, New Jersey, USA	4.0 (6.4)
Coney Island, New York, USA	3.0 (4.8)
FDR Boardwalk, New York, USA	2.5 (4.0)
Corkscrew Swamp Sanctuary, Florida, USA	2.3 (3.7)
Jarzoo Boardwalk, Sweden	2.0 (3.2)

219

state with the highest state capital elevation

New Mexico

Santa Fe, New Mexico, sits 7,000 feet (2133.6 m) above sea level. That's 1.3 miles (2.1 km) high! It's located in the southern end of the Rocky Mountains, in the foothills of the Sangre de Cristo mountain range. Founded in 1610, it is one of the oldest capital cities in the United States. The city is home to about 70,000 residents, making it the fourth most-populated city in the state. Santa Fe is known for its diverse arts community, and draws many tourists each year to its museums and festivals.

states with the highest state capital elevation

height above sea level, in feet (meters)

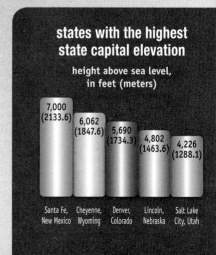

Santa Fe, New Mexico	Cheyenne, Wyoming	Denver, Colorado	Lincoln, Nebraska	Salt Lake City, Utah
7,000 (2133.6)	6,062 (1847.6)	5,690 (1734.3)	4,802 (1463.6)	4,226 (1288.1)

state with the most-visited art museum

New York

New York City's Metropolitan Museum of Art draws about 6 million visitors each year. It is also the largest art museum in the USA. The Met opened its doors on Fifth Avenue in March 1880, and has been expanding its building and growing its collections ever since. Today, the Met occupies a 2-million-square-foot (185,806 sq m) building, which contains about 2 million objects. Of these objects, tens of thousands are on display at any given time. Some of the popular areas of the museum include European Sculpture and Decorative Art, Greek and Roman Art, Egyptian Art, Asian Art, and the American Wing.

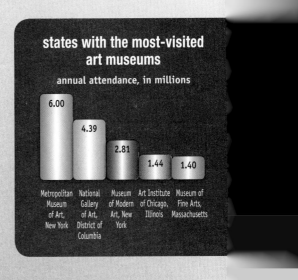

states with the most-visited art museums

annual attendance, in millions

6.00	4.39	2.81	1.44	1.40
Metropolitan Museum of Art, New York	National Gallery of Art, District of Columbia	Museum of Modern Art, New York	Art Institute of Chicago, Illinois	Museum of Fine Arts, Massachusetts

state with the tallest lighthouse

North Carolina

The Cape Hatteras lighthouse in North Carolina rises 200 feet (60.9 m) above the Atlantic Ocean. The lighthouse protects ships from a dangerous stretch of the Atlantic coast that includes a 12-mile (19.3 km) sandbar known as Diamond Shoals. The lighthouse was first lit in October 1870, and was assigned the distinctive black-and-white stripe pattern. Cape Hatteras lighthouse is open to the public during spring and summer, and visitors can climb its 248 iron stairs to the top. That's the equivalent of climbing a 12-story building. The lighthouse is maintained by the National Park Service.

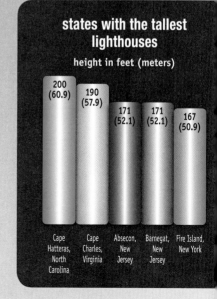

states with the tallest lighthouses

height in feet (meters)

200 (60.9)	190 (57.9)	171 (52.1)	171 (52.1)	167 (50.9)
Cape Hatteras, North Carolina	Cape Charles, Virginia	Absecon, New Jersey	Barnegat, New Jersey	Fire Island, New York

state with the tallest metal sculpture

North Dakota

In August 2001, Gary Greff created a 110-foot (33.5 m) tall metal sculpture along the stretch of road between Gladstone and Regent, North Dakota. That's the height of an 11-story building! The 154-foot (46.9 m) wide sculpture is called *Geese in Flight*, and shows Canada geese traveling across the prairie. Greff has created several other towering sculptures nearby, and the road has become known as the Enchanted Highway. He created these sculptures to attract tourists to the area and to support his hometown. He relies only on donations to finance his work.

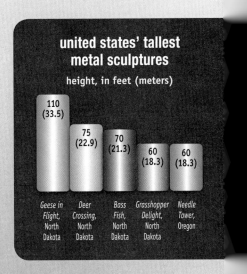

united states' tallest metal sculptures

height, in feet (meters)

Geese in Flight, North Dakota	Deer Crossing, North Dakota	Bass Fish, North Dakota	Grasshopper Delight, North Dakota	Needle Tower, Oregon
110 (33.5)	75 (22.9)	70 (21.3)	60 (18.3)	60 (18.3)

state with the world's largest twins gathering

Ohio

Each August, the town of Twinsburg, Ohio, hosts more than 4,100 twins at its annual Twins Day Festival. Both identical and fraternal twins from around the world participate, and many dress alike. The twins take part in games and contests, such as the oldest identical twins and the twins with the widest combined smile. There is also a Double Take parade, which is nationally televised. There are special twin programs for all age groups, since twins from ages 90 years to just 11 days old have attended. The event began in 1976 in honor of Aaron and Moses Wilcox, twin brothers who inspired the city to adopt its name in 1817.

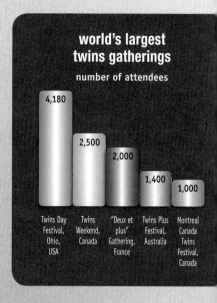

world's largest twins gatherings
number of attendees

Twins Day Festival, Ohio, USA	Twins Weekend, Canada	"Deux et plus" Gathering, France	Twins Plus Festival, Australia	Montreal Canada Twins Festival, Canada
4,180	2,500	2,000	1,400	1,000

state with the world's longest multiple-arch dam

Oklahoma

With a length of 6,565 feet (2,001 m), the Pensacola Dam in Oklahoma is the world's longest multiple-arch dam. Built in 1940, the dam is located on the Grand River and contains the Grand Lake o' the Cherokees—one of the largest reservoirs in the country, with 46,500 surface acres (18,818 ha) of water. The dam stands 145 feet (44 m) high. It was made out of 535,000 cubic yards of concrete, some 655,000 barrels of cement, another 10 million pounds (4.5 million kg) of structural steel, and 75,000 pounds (340,194 kg) of copper. The dam cost $27 million to complete.

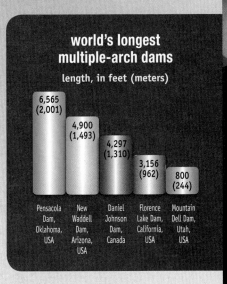

world's longest multiple-arch dams

length, in feet (meters)

Pensacola Dam, Oklahoma, USA	New Waddell Dam, Arizona, USA	Daniel Johnson Dam, Canada	Florence Lake Dam, California, USA	Mountain Dell Dam, Utah, USA
6,565 (2,001)	4,900 (1,493)	4,297 (1,310)	3,156 (962)	800 (244)

225

state with the deepest lake

Oregon

At a depth of 1,932 feet (589 m), Crater Lake in southern Oregon partially fills the remains of an old volcanic basin. The crater was formed almost 7,700 years ago when Mount Mazama erupted and then collapsed. The lake averages about 5 miles (8 km) in diameter. Crater Lake National Park—the nation's fifth-oldest park—surrounds the majestic lake and measures 249 square miles (645 sq km). The area's large snowfalls average 530 inches (1,346 cm) a year, and supply Crater Lake with its water. In addition to being the United States' deepest lake, it's also the eighth-deepest lake in the world.

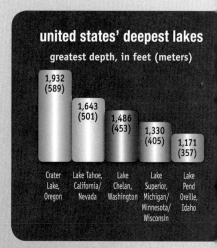

united states' deepest lakes

greatest depth, in feet (meters)

Crater Lake, Oregon	Lake Tahoe, California/ Nevada	Lake Chelan, Washington	Lake Superior, Michigan/ Minnesota/ Wisconsin	Lake Pend Oreille, Idaho
1,932 (589)	1,643 (501)	1,486 (453)	1,330 (405)	1,171 (357)

state with the oldest operating drive-in theater

Pennsylvania

Shankweiler's Drive-in Theatre opened in 1934. It was the country's second drive-in theater, and is the oldest one still operating today. Located in Orefield, Pennsylvania, the single-screen theater can accommodate 320 cars. Approximately 90 percent of the theater's guests are children. Although they originally used sound boxes located beside the cars, today's patrons can tune into a special radio station to hear the movies' music and dialogue. Shankweiler's is open from April to September.

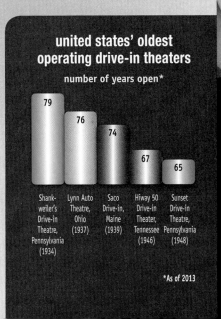

united states' oldest operating drive-in theaters

number of years open*

79				
	76			
		74		
			67	
				65
Shank-weiler's Drive-in Theatre, Pennsylvania (1934)	Lynn Auto Theatre, Ohio (1937)	Saco Drive-in, Maine (1939)	Hiway 50 Drive-in Theater, Tennessee (1946)	Sunset Drive-in Theatre, Pennsylvania (1948)

*As of 2013

227

state with the oldest temple

Rhode Island

The Touro Synagogue was dedicated during Hanukkah in December 1763 and is the oldest temple in the United States. Located in Newport, Rhode Island, the temple was designed by famous architect Peter Harrison and took four years to complete. In addition to serving as a symbol of religious freedom, the temple played another part in the country's history. When the British captured Newport in 1776, the temple briefly became a British hospital. Then, in 1781, George Washington met General Lafayette there to plan the final battles of the Revolution.

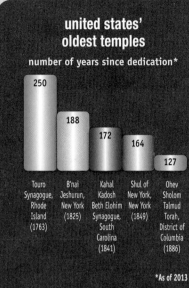

united states' oldest temples

number of years since dedication*

250	188	172	164	127
Touro Synagogue, Rhode Island (1763)	B'nai Jeshurun, New York (1825)	Kahal Kadosh Beth Elohim Synagogue, South Carolina (1841)	Shul of New York, New York (1849)	Ohev Sholom Talmud Torah, District of Columbia (1886)

*As of 2013

state with the oldest museum

South Carolina

The Charleston Museum in Charleston, South Carolina, was founded in 1773—three years before the Declaration of Independence was signed. The museum was founded to preserve the culture and history of the southern town and the surrounding area, and opened its doors to the public in 1824. Some of the exhibits in the museum include furniture, silver, and art made in the area, as well as fossils of local birds and animals. Two historic houses, which were built between 1772 and 1803, are also run by the museum. Visitors can tour these homes to learn about the state's early architecture.

united states' oldest museums

number of years open*

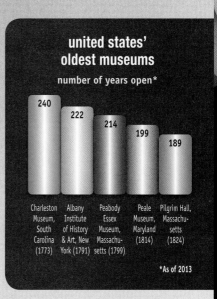

240	222	214	199	189
Charleston Museum, South Carolina (1773)	Albany Institute of History & Art, New York (1791)	Peabody Essex Museum, Massachusetts (1799)	Peale Museum, Maryland (1814)	Pilgrim Hall, Massachusetts (1824)

*As of 2013

229

state with the largest petrified wood collection

South Dakota

Lemmon's Petrified Wood Park in South Dakota is home to 30 acres (12.1 ha) of petrified wood. It covers an entire city block in downtown Lemmon. It was built between 1930 and 1932 when locals collected petrified wood from the area and constructed displays. One structure in the park—known as the Castle—weighs more than 300 tons (272 t) and is made partly from petrified wood and partly of petrified dinosaur and mammoth bones. Other exhibits include a wishing well, a waterfall, the Lemmon Pioneer Museum, and hundreds of pile sculptures.

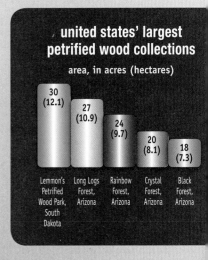

united states' largest petrified wood collections

area, in acres (hectares)

- 30 (12.1) — Lemmon's Petrified Wood Park, South Dakota
- 27 (10.9) — Long Logs Forest, Arizona
- 24 (9.7) — Rainbow Forest, Arizona
- 20 (8.1) — Crystal Forest, Arizona
- 18 (7.3) — Black Forest, Arizona

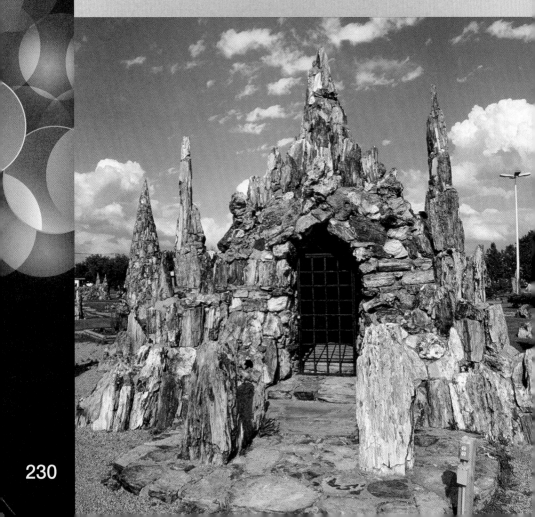

state with the world's largest freshwater aquarium

Tennessee

The Tennessee Aquarium in Chattanooga is an impressive 130,000 square feet (12,077 sq m), making it the largest freshwater aquarium in the world. The $45 million building holds a total of 400,000 gallons (1,514,165 L) of water. In addition, the aquarium features a 60,000-square-foot (5,574 sq m) building dedicated to the ocean and the creatures that live there. Permanent features in the aquarium include a discovery hall and an environmental learning lab. Some of the aquarium's 12,000 animals include baby alligators, paddlefish, lake sturgeon, sea dragons, and pipefish. And to feed all of these creatures, the aquarium goes through 12,000 crickets, 33,300 worms, and 1,200 pounds (545 kg) of seafood each month!

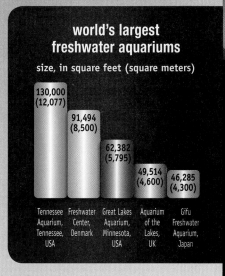

world's largest freshwater aquariums

size, in square feet (square meters)

130,000 (12,077)	91,494 (8,500)	62,382 (5,795)	49,514 (4,600)	46,285 (4,300)
Tennessee Aquarium, Tennessee, USA	Freshwater Center, Denmark	Great Lakes Aquarium, Minnesota, USA	Aquarium of the Lakes, UK	Gifu Freshwater Aquarium, Japan

state with the biggest ferris wheel

Texas

The State Fair of Texas boasts the nation's largest Ferris wheel. Called the Texas Star, this colossal wheel measures 212 feet (64.6 m) high. That's taller than a 20-story building! The Texas Star was built in Italy and shipped to Texas for its debut at the 1986 fair. Located in the 277-acre (112 ha) Fair Park, the Texas Star is just one of the 70 rides featured at the fair. The three-week-long State Fair of Texas is the biggest state fair in the country and brings in about $350 million in revenue annually. It is held in the fall, and the giant Ferris wheel is not the only grand-scale item there. Big Tex, a 52-foot (15.9 m) tall cowboy, is the fair's mascot and the tallest cowboy in the United States.

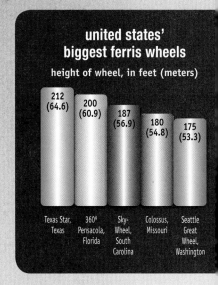

united states' biggest ferris wheels

height of wheel, in feet (meters)

Texas Star, Texas	360° Pensacola, Florida	Sky-Wheel, South Carolina	Colossus, Missouri	Seattle Great Wheel, Washington
212 (64.6)	200 (60.9)	187 (56.9)	180 (54.8)	175 (53.3)

state with the largest dinosaur collection

Utah

The Museum of Ancient Life at the Thanksgiving Point Institute in Lehi, Utah, has the largest dinosaur collection in the country with 60 complete skeletons on display. Guests are even invited to touch some of the real fossils, bones, and eggs that they are looking at. There are about 50 interactive displays throughout the Museum of Ancient Life. Guests touring the museum can also observe a working paleontology lab. The museum, which opened in June 2000, holds a sleepover once a month for kids to go on a behind-the-scenes tour.

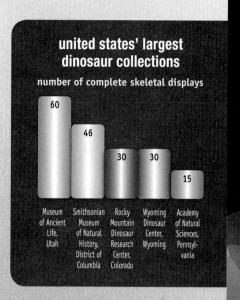

united states' largest dinosaur collections

number of complete skeletal displays

Museum of Ancient Life, Utah	Smithsonian Museum of Natural History, District of Columbia	Rocky Mountain Dinosaur Research Center, Colorado	Wyoming Dinosaur Center, Wyoming	Academy of Natural Sciences, Pennsylvania
60	46	30	30	15

state that produces the most maple syrup

Vermont

Maple syrup production in Vermont totaled more than 750,000 gallons (2,839,058 L) in 2012 and accounted for about 39 percent of the United States' total yield that year. There are approximately 3.2 million tree taps used by the state's 2,000 maple syrup producers, and the annual production generates almost $13.1 million. It takes about five tree taps to collect enough maple sap—approximately 40 gallons (151.4 L)—to produce just 1 gallon (3.79 L) of syrup. Vermont maple syrup is also made into maple sugar, maple cream, and maple candies.

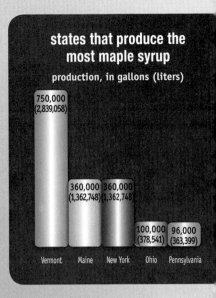

states that produce the most maple syrup

production, in gallons (liters)

750,000 (2,839,058)	360,000 (1,362,748)	360,000 (1,362,748)	100,000 (378,541)	96,000 (363,399)
Vermont	Maine	New York	Ohio	Pennsylvania

state with the largest office building

Virginia

The Pentagon Building in Arlington, Virginia, measures 6,636,360 square feet (616,538 sq m) and covers 583 acres (236 ha). In fact, the US Capitol can fit inside the building five times! Although the Pentagon contains 17.5 miles (28.2 km) of hallways, the design of the building allows people to reach any destination in about seven minutes. The Pentagon is almost like a small city, employing about 23,000 people. About 200,000 phone calls are made there daily, and the internal post office handles an average of 1.2 million pieces of mail each month.

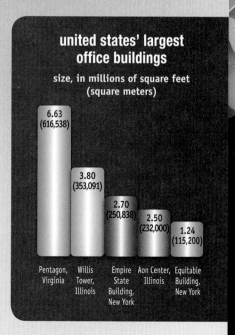

united states' largest office buildings

size, in millions of square feet (square meters)

Building	Size
Pentagon, Virginia	6.63 (616,538)
Willis Tower, Illinois	3.80 (353,091)
Empire State Building, New York	2.70 (250,838)
Aon Center, Illinois	2.50 (232,000)
Equitable Building, New York	1.24 (115,200)

235

state with the longest train tunnel

Washington

The Cascade Tunnel runs through the Cascade Mountains in central Washington and measures 7.8 miles (12.6 km) long. The tunnel connects the towns of Berne and Scenic. It was built by the Great Northern Railway in 1929 to replace the original tunnel, which was built at an elevation frequently hit with snowslides. To help cool the trains' diesel engines and remove fumes, the tunnel is equipped with huge fans that blow air while and after a train passes.

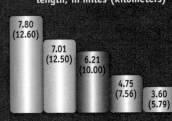

united states' longest train tunnels

length, in miles (kilometers)

Cascade Tunnel, Washington	Flathead Tunnel, Missouri	Moffat Tunnel, Colorado	Hoosac Tunnel, Massachusetts	BART Transbay Tube, California
7.80 (12.60)	7.01 (12.50)	6.21 (10.00)	4.75 (7.56)	3.60 (5.79)

CASCADE TUNNEL
7.8 MILES LONG   ELEVATION 2,247 FEET
41,152 FEET LONG   COMPLETED 1928

state with the longest steel arch bridge

West Virginia

With a main span of 1,700 feet (518 m) and a weight of about 88 million pounds (40 million kg), the New River Gorge Bridge in Fayetteville, West Virginia, is the longest and largest steel arch bridge in the United States. It is approximately 875 feet (267 m) above the New River and is the second-highest bridge in the country. After three years of construction, the bridge was completed in 1977. The $37 million structure is the focus of Bridge Day—a statewide annual festival that is one of the largest extreme sports events in the United States, drawing hundreds of BASE jumpers and thousands of spectators.

united states' longest steel arch bridges

length of main span, in feet (meters)

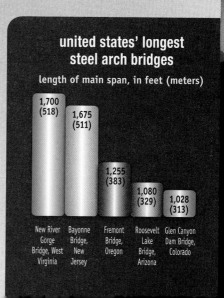

New River Gorge Bridge, West Virginia	Bayonne Bridge, New Jersey	Fremont Bridge, Oregon	Roosevelt Lake Bridge, Arizona	Glen Canyon Dam Bridge, Colorado
1,700 (518)	1,675 (511)	1,255 (383)	1,080 (329)	1,028 (313)

237

state that produces the most cranberries

Wisconsin

Wisconsin harvested more than 4.8 million barrels of cranberries in 2012. That's 60 percent of all cranberries grown in the United States. Wisconsin's cranberry crop was worth more than $230 million. In all, the state harvests about 19,700 acres (7,972 ha). About 130,000 barrels of the berries were sold fresh, while the rest were processed into juices, sauce, and other products. Wisconsin farmers began cultivating cranberries in the 1860s, and they are currently grown in 19 of the state's 72 counties.

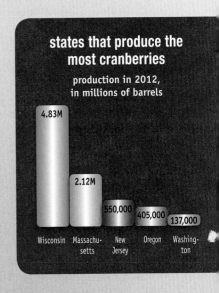

states that produce the most cranberries

production in 2012, in millions of barrels

Wisconsin	Massachu-setts	New Jersey	Oregon	Washing-ton
4.83M	2.12M	550,000	405,000	137,000

state that produces the most coal

Wyoming

Wyoming produced 400 million tons (362.8 million t) of coal in 2012—about 40 percent of the nation's total. Of the top-ten coal-producing mines in the United States, nine of them are in Wyoming. In fact, the top two mines—North Antelope Rochelle and Black Thunder—produce 20 percent of the country's coal. North Antelope Rochelle mine produced 108 million tons (97.9 million t), and Black Thunder contributed 93 million tons (84.3 million t). Wyoming's top ten mines are all located along the Powder River Basin. Wyoming has about a 42-billion-ton (38.1 billion t) reserve of recoverable coal.

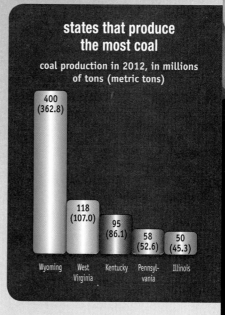

states that produce the most coal

coal production in 2012, in millions of tons (metric tons)

Wyoming	400 (362.8)
West Virginia	118 (107.0)
Kentucky	95 (86.1)
Pennsylvania	58 (52.6)
Illinois	50 (45.3)

Sports Records

Amazing Attendance Accomplishment

The Boston Red Sox had maximum attendance for 820 games between May 2003 and April 2013, setting the MLB record for the longest consecutive sell-out streak. The previous longest sell-out streak in sports was 814 games held by the NBA's Portland Trail Blazers.

Boxing Brings in Bucks

Boxer Floyd Mayweather, Jr. is the highest-paid athlete in the United States. During 2013, he earned $90 million from his fights. Mayweather, Jr. has won eight world titles, and picked up a bronze medal at the 1996 Atlanta Games. Mayweather, Jr. had his first professional fight in 1996, and has won 44 consecutive bouts since then.

Cabrera's Crown

During 2012, Detroit Tiger Miguel Cabrera was on top of his game when he earned baseball's Triple Crown. He not only led the American League in batting average (.330), home runs (44), and runs batted in (139), the third-baseman also took home the AL Most Valuable Player Award that year.

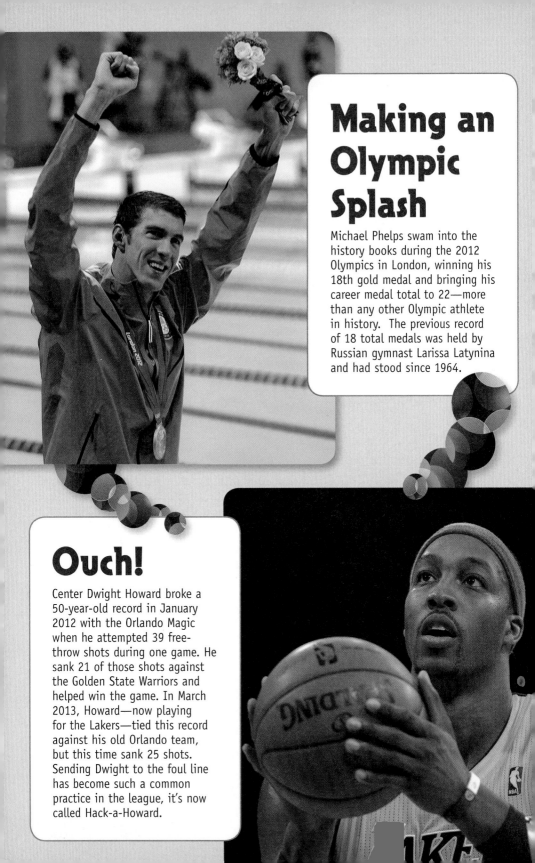

Making an Olympic Splash

Michael Phelps swam into the history books during the 2012 Olympics in London, winning his 18th gold medal and bringing his career medal total to 22—more than any other Olympic athlete in history. The previous record of 18 total medals was held by Russian gymnast Larissa Latynina and had stood since 1964.

Ouch!

Center Dwight Howard broke a 50-year-old record in January 2012 with the Orlando Magic when he attempted 39 free-throw shots during one game. He sank 21 of those shots against the Golden State Warriors and helped win the game. In March 2013, Howard—now playing for the Lakers—tied this record against his old Orlando team, but this time sank 25 shots. Sending Dwight to the foul line has become such a common practice in the league, it's now called Hack-a-Howard.

Supersonic Speed

Usain Bolt proved he is truly the fastest man in the world when he won gold in both the 100m and 200m sprints at the 2012 Olympic Games. Bolt—who is the first runner ever to achieve this—completed the 100m in 9.63 seconds and the 200m in just 19.32 seconds.

Right on Target

In 2012, the New Orleans Saints' Drew Brees became the quarterback with the most consecutive games completing a touchdown pass—he surpassed Johnny Unitas's 1960 record of 47. Brees's streak began during week 4 of the 2009 season, and ended in November 2012 with a total of 54 completed touchdown passes.

nba team with the most championship titles

Boston Celtics

The Boston Celtics are the most successful team in the NBA with 17 championship wins. The first win came in 1957, and the team went on to win the next seven consecutive titles—the longest streak of consecutive championship wins in the history of US sports. The most recent championship title came in 2008. The Celtics entered the Basketball Association of America in 1946, which later merged into the NBA in 1949. The Celtics made the NBA play-offs for four consecutive seasons from 2001 to 2005, but they were eliminated in early rounds each time.

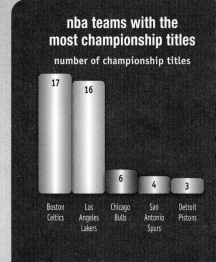

nba teams with the most championship titles

number of championship titles

Boston Celtics	Los Angeles Lakers	Chicago Bulls	San Antonio Spurs	Detroit Pistons
17	16	6	4	3

nba player with the highest career scoring average

Wilt Chamberlain & Michael Jordan

Both Michael Jordan and Wilt Chamberlain averaged an amazing 30.1 points per game during their legendary careers. Jordan played for the Chicago Bulls and the Washington Wizards. He led the league in scoring for seven years. During the 1986 season, he became the second person ever to score 3,000 points in a single season. Chamberlain played for the Philadelphia Warriors, the Philadelphia 76ers, and the Los Angeles Lakers. In addition to the highest scoring average, he holds the record for the most games with 50 or more points, with 118.

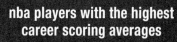

nba players with the highest career scoring averages

average points per game

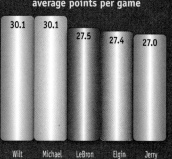

Wilt Chamberlain, 1959–1973	Michael Jordan, 1984–1998; 2001–2003	LeBron James, 2003–	Elgin Baylor, 1958–1971	Jerry West, 1960–1974
30.1	30.1	27.5	27.4	27.0

Michael Jordan

245

nba's highest-scoring game

Detroit Pistons

On December 13, 1983, the Detroit Pistons beat the Denver Nuggets with a score of 186–184 at McNichols Arena in Denver, Colorado. The game was tied at 145 at the end of regular play, and three overtime periods were needed to determine the winner. During the game, both the Pistons and the Nuggets each had six players who scored in the double figures. Four players scored more than 40 points each, which was an NBA first. The Pistons scored 74 field goals that night, claiming another NBA record that still stands today.

nba's highest-scoring games
points scored by a team in one game

186	184	173	173	171
Detroit Pistons, vs. Denver Nuggets, 1983	Denver Nuggets, vs. Detroit Pistons, 1983	Boston Celtics, vs. Minneapolis Lakers, 1959	Phoenix Suns, vs. Denver Nuggets, 1990	San Antonio Spurs, vs. Milwaukee Bucks, 1982

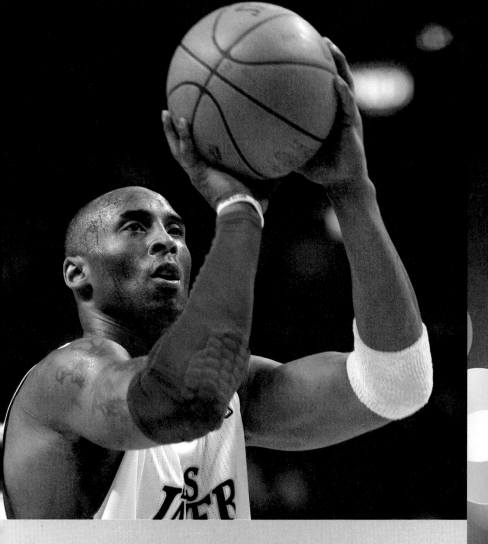

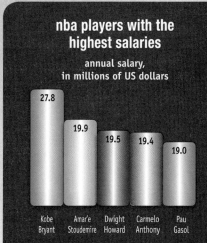

nba player with the highest salary

Kobe Bryant

Kobe Bryant earns $27.8 million a year playing as a guard for the LA Lakers. Bryant has been a Laker since he turned pro in 1996. During his 15 years in the NBA, he has scored more than 29,440 points and grabbed more than 6,100 rebounds. Bryant has also logged almost 42,200 minutes on the court. He was a five-time NBA Champion, between 2000 and 2010, and he was the NBA Most Valuable Player during the 2007–2008 season. He has also earned All-NBA honors every year since 2002. In 2008, Bryant helped Team USA win the gold medal at the Beijing Olympics.

nba players with the highest salaries

annual salary,
in millions of US dollars

Kobe Bryant	Amar'e Stoudemire	Dwight Howard	Carmelo Anthony	Pau Gasol
27.8	19.9	19.5	19.4	19.0

247

nba player with the highest field goal percentage

Artis Gilmore

Artis Gilmore leads the NBA with the highest career field goal percentage at .599. He was drafted by the Chicago Bulls in 1971, and went on to also play for the San Antonio Spurs and the Boston Celtics before retiring in 1988. A center who towered more than 7 feet (2 m) tall, Gilmore had 9,161 rebounds and 1,747 blocks. He also scored 15,579 points and had 1,777 assists. He was a five-time NBA All Star between 1978 and 1986. Gilmore, who was nicknamed the A-Train, played 909 regular season games.

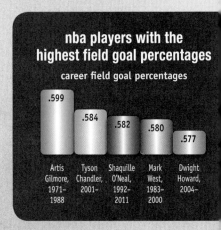

nba players with the highest field goal percentages

career field goal percentages

Artis Gilmore, 1971–1988	Tyson Chandler, 2001–	Shaquille O'Neal, 1992–2011	Mark West, 1983–2000	Dwight Howard, 2004–
.599	.584	.582	.580	.577

nba player with the most career points

Kareem Abdul-Jabbar

During his highly successful career, Kareem Abdul-Jabbar scored a total of 38,387 points. In 1969, Abdul-Jabbar began his NBA tenure with the Milwaukee Bucks. He was named Rookie of the Year in 1970. The following year he scored 2,596 points and helped the Bucks win the NBA championship. He was traded to the Los Angeles Lakers in 1975, and with his new team, Abdul-Jabbar won the NBA championship in 1980, 1982, 1985, 1987, and 1988. He retired from basketball in 1989 and was inducted into the Basketball Hall of Fame in 1995.

nba players with the most career points

points scored

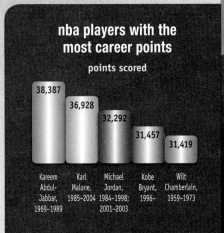

38,387	36,928	32,292	31,457	31,419
Kareem Abdul-Jabbar, 1969–1989	Karl Malone, 1985–2004	Michael Jordan, 1984–1998; 2001–2003	Kobe Bryant, 1996–	Wilt Chamberlain, 1959–1973

wnba player with the highest career ppg average

Cynthia Cooper

Cynthia Cooper has the highest scoring average in the WNBA with 21 points per game. During the play-offs, she has averaged 23.3 points per game. Cooper joined the league in 1997 as a Houston Comet and remained there for four years. After a two-year hiatus, she returned for a year, and then retired in 2003. During her five years in the WNBA, she scored a total of 2,601 points. Cooper has a career high of 44 points in one game versus Sacramento in 1997. She won a gold medal in the 1988 Olympics in Seoul, the 1987 Pan American Games, and the 1990 FIBA World Championship.

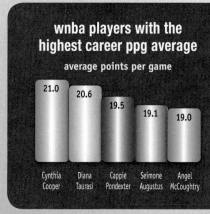

wnba players with the highest career ppg average

average points per game

Cynthia Cooper	Diana Taurasi	Cappie Pondexter	Seimone Augustus	Angel McCoughtry
21.0	20.6	19.5	19.1	19.0

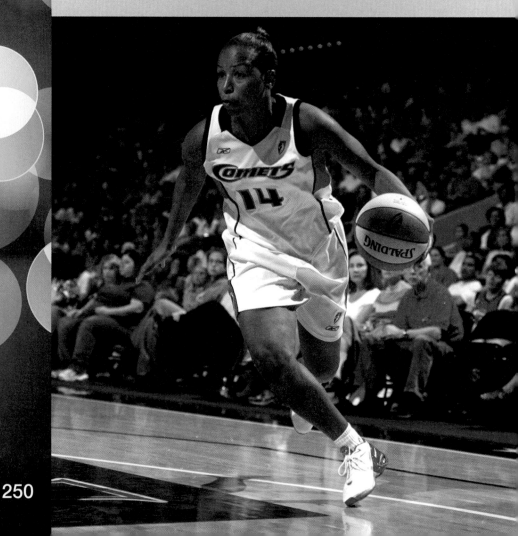

wnba player with the highest free-throw percentage

Lynetta Kizer

Lynetta Kizer has a free-throw percentage of .935. Kizer was selected by the Tulsa Shock in the third round of the 2012 draft. After playing seven games for the Shock, Kizer was waived, and she was signed by the Phoenix Mercury. During her first season in the WNBA, Kizer played in 22 games, scored 125 points, and grabbed 66 rebounds. The 6-foot-4-inch (1.9 m) center played for the University of Maryland before turning pro. She was the Atlantic Coast Conference Rookie of the Year in 2009, and was named to the first team All-ACC Tournament in 2012.

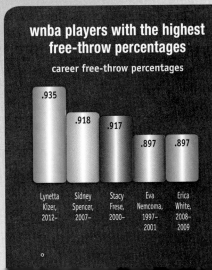

wnba players with the highest free-throw percentages

career free-throw percentages

Lynetta Kizer, 2012–	Sidney Spencer, 2007–	Stacy Frese, 2000–	Eva Nemcoma, 1997–2001	Erica White, 2008–2009
.935	.918	.917	.897	.897

wnba player with the most career points

Tina Thompson

A nine-time WNBA All-Star, Tina Thompson has scored 7,009 points during her 16-year career. The Los Angeles Sparks forward began her WNBA career in 1997 with the Houston Comets. She was the first draft pick in WNBA history. During her first four years with the Comets, she helped the team win the WNBA Championship each season and was the 2000 All-Star MVP. She joined the Los Angeles Sparks in 2009, and has a points-per-game average of 15.1. At the 2004 and 2008 Olympic Games, Thompson picked up gold medals for her role in helping Team USA dominate the competition.

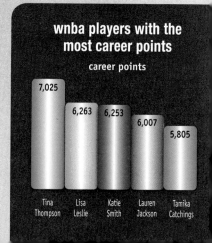

wnba players with the most career points

career points

Tina Thompson	Lisa Leslie	Katie Smith	Lauren Jackson	Tamika Catchings
7,025	6,263	6,253	6,007	5,805

WNBA player with the most career rebounds

Lisa Leslie

Lisa Leslie grabbed 3,307 rebounds during her 12-year career in the WNBA. Leslie joined the league during its inaugural season in 1997 when she was signed by the Los Angeles Sparks. Leslie remained with the team throughout her career. A three-time WNBA MVP and eight-time WNBA All Star, Leslie became the first woman to dunk in the league in 2002. In 2009, she again made history by becoming the first woman to score 6,000 points. Leslie won four Olympic gold medals between 1996 and 2008.

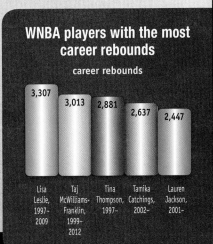

WNBA players with the most career rebounds

career rebounds

3,307	3,013	2,881	2,637	2,447
Lisa Leslie, 1997–2009	Taj McWilliams-Franklin, 1999–2012	Tina Thompson, 1997–	Tamika Catchings, 2002–	Lauren Jackson, 2001–

Tennessee & UCONN

The Tennessee Lady Volunteers and the UCONN Huskies have each won eight NCAA basketball championships. The Lady Vols won their trophies between 1987 and 2008, all under the leadership of head coach Pat Summitt. In 1998, they had a perfect record of 39–0, which was the most seasonal wins ever in women's collegiate basketball at the time. The Huskies won their championships between 1995 and 2013, all under the leadership of head coach Geno Auriemma. Connecticut also holds the records for the longest consecutive games won in the NCAA with 90 between April 2008 and December 2010.

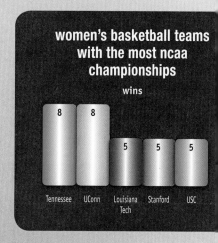

women's basketball teams with the most ncaa championships

wins

Tennessee	UConn	Louisiana Tech	Stanford	USC
8	8	5	5	5

men's basketball team with the most ncaa championships

UCLA

With 11 titles, the University of California, Los Angeles (UCLA) has the most NCAA basketball championship wins. The Bruins won their 11th championship in 1995. The school has won 23 of their last 41 league titles and has been in the NCAA play-offs for 35 of the last 41 years. During the final round of the NCAA championship in 2006, UCLA lost to the Florida Gators with a score of 73–57. Not surprisingly, UCLA has produced some basketball legends, including Kareem Abdul-Jabbar, Reggie Miller, and Baron Davis. For the last 36 years, the Bruins have called Pauley Pavilion home.

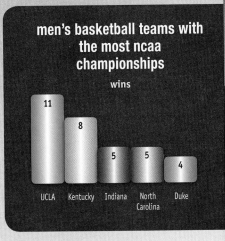

men's basketball teams with the most ncaa championships

wins

UCLA	Kentucky	Indiana	North Carolina	Duke
11	8	5	5	4

nfl player with the most passing yards

Brett Favre

Quarterback Brett Favre knows how to hit his receivers: He completed 71,838 passing yards during his amazing career. He has a completion rate of 62 percent, and has connected for 508 touchdowns. Favre is also the NFL's all-time leader in passing touchdowns (508), completions (6,300), and attempts (10,169). Favre began his career with the Atlanta Falcons in 1991. He was traded to the Green Bay Packers the next season, and played for them until 2007. Favre joined the New York Jets for the season, and was then signed by the Minnesota Vikings for the 2009 season.

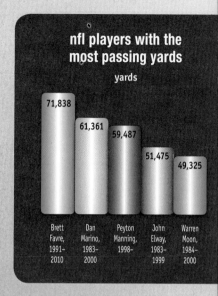

nfl players with the most passing yards
yards

Brett Favre, 1991–2010	Dan Marino, 1983–2000	Peyton Manning, 1998–	John Elway, 1983–1999	Warren Moon, 1984–2000
71,838	61,361	59,487	51,475	49,325

nfl player with the highest career rushing total

Emmitt Smith

Running back Emmitt Smith holds the record for all-time rushing yards with 18,355. Smith began his career with the Dallas Cowboys in 1990 and played with the team until the end of the 2002 season. In 2003, Smith signed a two-year contract with the Arizona Cardinals. Smith also holds the NFL records for the most carries with 4,142 and the most rushing touchdowns with 164. After 15 years in the NFL, Smith retired at the end of the 2004 season.

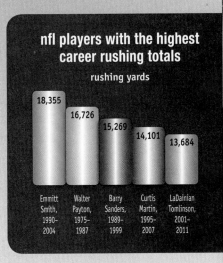

nfl players with the highest career rushing totals

rushing yards

Emmitt Smith, 1990–2004	Walter Payton, 1975–1987	Barry Sanders, 1989–1999	Curtis Martin, 1995–2007	LaDainian Tomlinson, 2001–2011
18,355	16,726	15,269	14,101	13,684

nfl player with the most career touchdowns

Jerry Rice

Jerry Rice has scored a record 208 touchdowns. He is widely considered to be one of the greatest wide receivers to ever play in the National Football League. Rice holds a total of 14 NFL records, including career receptions (1,549), receiving yards (22,895), receiving touchdowns (197), most games with 100 receiving yards (75), and many others. He was named NFL Player of the Year twice, *Sports Illustrated* Player of the Year four times, and NFL Offensive Player of the Year once. Rice retired from the NFL in 2005.

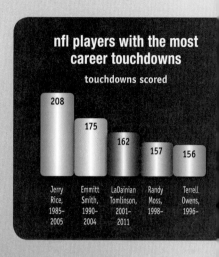

nfl players with the most career touchdowns

touchdowns scored

208	175	162	157	156
Jerry Rice, 1985–2005	Emmitt Smith, 1990–2004	LaDainian Tomlinson, 2001–2011	Randy Moss, 1998–	Terrell Owens, 1996–

nfl player with the most single-season touchdowns

LaDainian Tomlinson

Running back LaDainian Tomlinson scored 31 touchdowns during the 2006 season. He was also named NFL Most Valuable Player that season for his outstanding performance. During his pro career, he has scored a total of 138 touchdowns. Tomlinson was selected fifth overall in the 2001 draft by the San Diego Chargers but was traded to the New York Jets in 2010. He holds several Chargers records, including 372 attempts (2002), 100 receptions (2003), and 1,815 rushing yards in a season (2006). Tomlinson has also been named to five Pro Bowls.

nfl players with the most single-season touchdowns

touchdowns scored

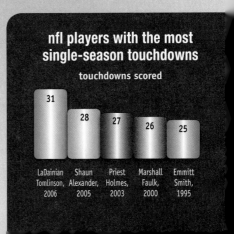

LaDainian Tomlinson, 2006	Shaun Alexander, 2005	Priest Holmes, 2003	Marshall Faulk, 2000	Emmitt Smith, 1995
31	28	27	26	25

nfl player with the highest career scoring total

Morten Andersen

Morten Andersen led the NFL in scoring with a career total of 2,544 points. He made 565 field goals out of 709 attempts, giving him a 79.7 percent completion rate. He scored 849 extra points out of 859 attempts, resulting in a 98.8 percent success rate. Andersen, a placekicker who began his career in 1982 with the New Orleans Saints, retired in 2008 after playing for the Atlanta Falcons. Known as the Great Dane, partly because of his birthplace of Denmark, Andersen played 382 professional games. His most successful season was in 1995, when he scored 122 points.

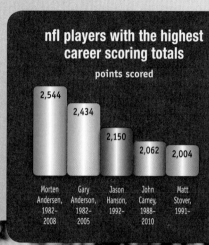

nfl players with the highest career scoring totals

points scored

Morten Andersen, 1982–2008	Gary Anderson, 1982–2005	Jason Hanson, 1992–	John Carney, 1988–2010	Matt Stover, 1991–
2,544	2,434	2,150	2,062	2,004

nfl player with the most quarterback sacks

Bruce Smith

During his 19 seasons in the NFL, defensive end Bruce Smith managed to sack the opposing quarterback 200 times. Smith was the first overall draft pick by the Buffalo Bills in 1985, and played for them until he was traded to the Washington Redskins in 2000. He was selected for the Pro Bowl 11 times and the First Team All Pro 9 times between 1987 and 1998. Smith was a four-time AFC Champion, and was named AP Defensive Player of the Year twice. He was also a part of the 1980s and 1990s All-Decade teams. Smith was inducted into the Pro Football Hall of Fame in 2009.

nfl players with the most quarterback sacks

career sacks

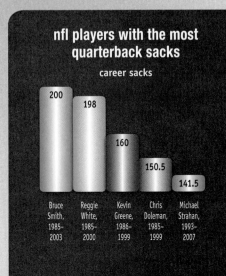

Bruce Smith, 1985–2003	Reggie White, 1985–2000	Kevin Greene, 1986–1999	Chris Doleman, 1985–1999	Michael Strahan, 1993–2007
200	198	160	150.5	141.5

nfl coach with the most wins

Don Shula

Don Shula led his teams to a remarkable 347 wins during his 33 years as a head coach in the National Football League. When Shula became head coach of the Baltimore Colts in 1963, he became the youngest head coach in football history. He stayed with the team until 1969 and reached the play-offs four times. Shula became the head coach for the Miami Dolphins in 1970 and coached them until 1995. During this time, the Dolphins reached the play-offs 20 times and won at least 10 games a season 21 times. After leading them to Super Bowl wins in 1972 and 1973, Shula became one of only five coaches to win the championship in back-to-back years.

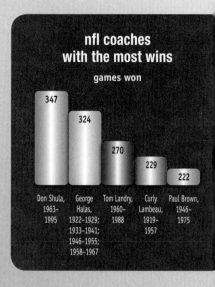

nfl coaches with the most wins

games won

Don Shula, 1963–1995	George Halas, 1922–1929; 1933–1941; 1946–1955; 1958–1967	Tom Landry, 1960–1988	Curly Lambeau, 1919–1957	Paul Brown, 1946–1975
347	324	270	229	222

highest paid football player

Aaron Rodgers

During 2013, Green Bay Packers quarterback Aaron Rodgers signed a five-year, $110 million deal, paying out a record $22 million a year. He also rakes in millions with endorsement deals for Pizza Hut, Nike, and State Farm. Rodgers has a career quarterback rating of 104.9, a completion rate of 65.7 percent, and a total of 21,661 passing yards. In the 2010 season, Rodgers led his team to victory during Super Bowl XLV and was named the game's MVP. He was also named the Associated Press Athlete of the Year in 2011. Rodgers was drafted by the Packers in 2005, and became their starting quarterback in 2008.

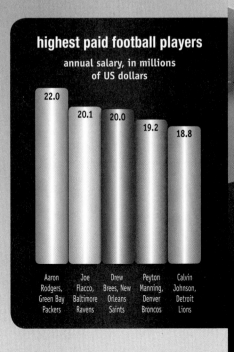

highest paid football players
annual salary, in millions of US dollars

Aaron Rodgers, Green Bay Packers	Joe Flacco, Baltimore Ravens	Drew Brees, New Orleans Saints	Peyton Manning, Denver Broncos	Calvin Johnson, Detroit Lions
22.0	20.1	20.0	19.2	18.8

NFL quarterback with the highest seasonal rating

Aaron Rodgers

During 2012, Aaron Rodgers had the highest quarterback rating in the NFL with 108.0. His career rating is 104.9, with 21,661 passing yards and 171 touchdowns. He holds the record for the lowest pass interception percentage with 1.7 percent. Rodgers signed with the Green Bay Packers in 2005 and has remained with the team throughout his career. He became the team's starting quarterback in 2008. In 2011, he led the team to a Super Bowl victory and was named Super Bowl MVP. He was also the Associated Press Athlete of the Year in 2011.

NFL quarterbacks with the highest seasonal rating
rating in 2012

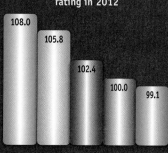

Aaron Rodgers, 2005–	Peyton Manning, 1998–	Robert Griffin III, 2012–	Russell Wilson, 2012–	Matt Ryan, 2008–
108.0	105.8	102.4	100.0	99.1

nfl team with the most super bowl wins

Pittsburgh Steelers

With six championship wins between 1974 and 2009, the Pittsburgh Steelers have won more Super Bowls than any other team in NFL history. The Steelers have also played and won more AFC championship games than any other team in the conference. The Steelers were founded in 1933 and are the fifth-oldest franchise in the league. Twenty-three retired Steelers have been inducted into the Pro Football Hall of Fame, including Franco Harris, Chuck Noll, and Terry Bradshaw.

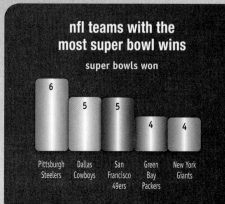

nfl teams with the most super bowl wins

super bowls won

Pittsburgh Steelers	Dallas Cowboys	San Francisco 49ers	Green Bay Packers	New York Giants
6	5	5	4	4

265

most valuable sporting event prize

UEFA Champions League

The UEFA Champions League—also known as the European Cup—awards the winning soccer team $77 million in prize money. The annual competition began in 1955 for the winning soccer team of each European country, but today countries can send up to four teams to compete. The main tournament includes 32 teams that are divided into eight groups. The winner of the UEFA Champions League qualifies for the FIFA Club World Cup. Real Madrid holds the record for most victories with nine wins. Twenty-two teams have won the big game, and twelve have won it more than once. The final game is extremely popular in Europe, drawing a television audience of about 170 million.

most valuable sporting events prizes

prize money paid to the winning team, in millions of US dollars

77.0	33.0	31.0	15.5	14.8
UEFA Champions League	UEFA European Football Championship	FIFA World Cup	Super Bowl	World Series

pga golfer with the lowest seasonal average

Rory McIlroy

Rory McIlroy's seasonal average was 68.87 in 2012—the lowest in the PGA. At the end of that year, McIlroy was named PGA Tour Player of the Year. The Irish golfer, who turned pro in 2007, has won more than $13.5 million in prize money. He's won 6 PGA Tour tournaments, including the Wells Fargo Championship, the US Open, The Honda Classic, The PGA Championship, the Deutsche Bank Championship, and the BMW Championship. Out of the 58 tournaments he's played, McIlroy has finished among the top ten players 23 times.

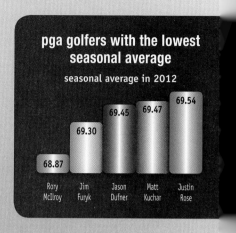

pga golfers with the lowest seasonal average

seasonal average in 2012

Rory McIlroy	Jim Furyk	Jason Dufner	Matt Kuchar	Justin Rose
68.87	69.30	69.45	69.47	69.54

lpga golfer with the lowest seasonal average

Inbee Park

Inbee Park led the LPGA in 2012 with a seasonal average of 70.21. In addition to winning the Vare Trophy for this accomplishment, Park also made the cut in 23 of her 24 events for the year. She won 2 tournaments, had 6 runner-up finishes, and had 10 additional top-ten finishes. Park had 347 birdies and 10 eagles for the year, as well as 72.3 percent of her rounds under par. Since turning pro in 2006, Park has won more than $6 million. In 2008, she was the youngest player to win the US Open at the age of 19 years, 11 months, and 17 days.

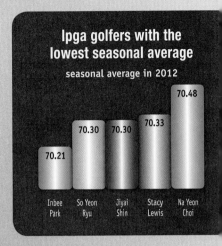

lpga golfers with the lowest seasonal average

seasonal average in 2012

Inbee Park	So Yeon Ryu	Jiyai Shin	Stacy Lewis	Na Yeon Choi
70.21	70.30	70.30	70.33	70.48

lpga's highest-paid golfer

Annika Sorenstam

Annika Sorenstam has earned $22.5 million since her LPGA career began in 1994. During this time, she has had 72 career victories, including ten majors. In 2005, Sorenstam earned her eighth Rolex Player of the Year award—the most in LPGA history. She also became the first player to sweep Rolex Player of the Year honors, the Vare Trophy, and the ADT Official Money List title five times. Sorenstam earned her fifth consecutive Mizuno Classic title, making her the first golfer in LPGA history to win the same event five consecutive years. Sorenstam retired at the end of the 2008 season.

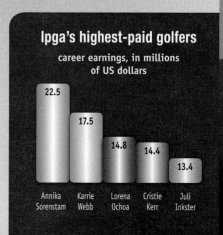

lpga's highest-paid golfers

career earnings, in millions of US dollars

Annika Sorenstam	Karrie Webb	Lorena Ochoa	Cristie Kerr	Juli Inkster
22.5	17.5	14.8	14.4	13.4

golfer with the most major tournament wins

Jack Nicklaus

Golfing great Jack Nicklaus has won a total of 18 major championships. His wins include six Masters, five PGAs, four US Opens, and three British Opens. Nicklaus was named PGA Player of the Year five times. He was a member of the winning US Ryder Cup team six times and was an individual World Cup winner a record three times. He was inducted into the World Golf Hall of Fame in 1974, just 12 years after he turned professional. He joined the US Senior PGA Tour in 1990. In addition to playing the game, Nicklaus has designed close to 200 golf courses and has written a number of popular books about the sport.

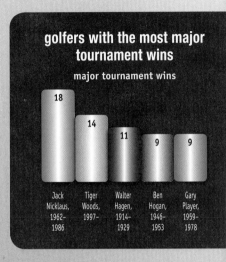

golfers with the most major tournament wins

major tournament wins

Jack Nicklaus, 1962–1986	Tiger Woods, 1997–	Walter Hagen, 1914–1929	Ben Hogan, 1946–1953	Gary Player, 1959–1978
18	14	11	9	9

mlb player with the highest seasonal home-run total

Barry Bonds

On October 5, 2001, Barry Bonds smashed Mark McGwire's record for seasonal home runs when he hit his 71st home run in the first inning of a game against the Los Angeles Dodgers. In the third inning, he hit number 72, and two days later he reached 73. Bonds, a left fielder for the San Francisco Giants, has a career total of 762 home runs. He also holds the records for seasonal walks (232) and seasonal on-base percentage (.609). Bonds and his father, hitting coach Bobby Bonds, hold the all-time father-son home-run record with 1,020.

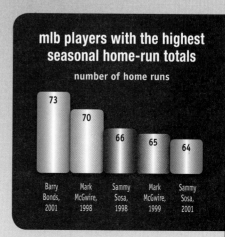

mlb players with the highest seasonal home-run totals

number of home runs

Barry Bonds, 2001	Mark McGwire, 1998	Sammy Sosa, 1998	Mark McGwire, 1999	Sammy Sosa, 2001
73	70	66	65	64

mlb team with the highest payroll

New York Yankees

The combined 2013 payroll of the New York Yankees totaled more than $230 million. Some of the highest-paid players include Alex Rodriguez ($30 million), C. C. Sabathia ($23 million), and Mark Teixeira ($23.1 million). The Yankees have been very successful with their pricey roster, winning 40 American League pennants and 27 World Series. The team also has a new place to showcase its talent—a new Yankee Stadium opened in 2009. The stadium cost $1.5 billion, making it the second-most expensive stadium in the world.

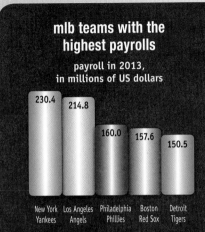

mlb teams with the highest payrolls

payroll in 2013, in millions of US dollars

New York Yankees	Los Angeles Angels	Philadelphia Phillies	Boston Red Sox	Detroit Tigers
230.4	214.8	160.0	157.6	150.5

mlb player with the most home runs

Barry Bonds

Barry Bonds has hit more home runs than anyone who ever played in the MLB, cracking 762 balls over the wall during his ongoing career. Bonds has hit more than 30 home runs in a season 14 times—another MLB record. During his impressive career, Bonds has won 8 Gold Gloves, 12 Silver Slugger awards, and 14 All-Star games. Bonds began his career with the Pittsburgh Pirates in 1986; he was transferred to the San Francisco Giants in 1993 and played for the team until he retired. He is only one of three players to join the 700 Home Run Club.

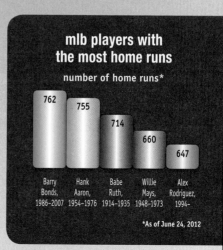

mlb players with the most home runs

number of home runs*

Barry Bonds, 1986–2007	Hank Aaron, 1954–1976	Babe Ruth, 1914–1935	Willie Mays, 1948–1973	Alex Rodriguez, 1994–
762	755	714	660	647

*As of June 24, 2012

273

mlb pitcher with the most career strikeouts

Nolan Ryan

Nolan Ryan leads Major League Baseball with an incredible 5,714 career strikeouts. In his impressive 27-season career, he played for the New York Mets, the California Angels, the Houston Astros, and the Texas Rangers. The right-handed pitcher from Refugio, Texas, led the American League in strikeouts ten times. In 1989, at the age of 42, Ryan became the oldest pitcher ever to lead the Major Leagues in strikeouts. Ryan set another record in 1991 when he pitched his seventh career no-hitter.

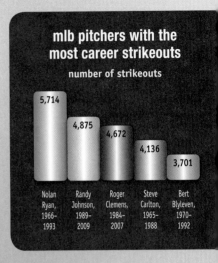

mlb pitchers with the most career strikeouts
number of strikeouts

Pitcher	Strikeouts
Nolan Ryan, 1966–1993	5,714
Randy Johnson, 1989–2009	4,875
Roger Clemens, 1984–2007	4,672
Steve Carlton, 1965–1988	4,136
Bert Blyleven, 1970–1992	3,701

mlb player with the most career hits

Pete Rose

Pete Rose belted an amazing 4,256 hits during his 23 years of professional baseball. He made his record-setting hit in 1985, when he was a player-manager for the Cincinnati Reds. By the time Rose retired as a player from Major League Baseball in 1986, he had set several other career records. Rose holds the Major League records for the most career games (3,562), the most times at bat (14,053), and the most seasons with more than 200 hits (10). During his career, he played for the Cincinnati Reds, the Philadelphia Phillies, and the Montreal Expos.

mlb players with the most career hits

number of hits

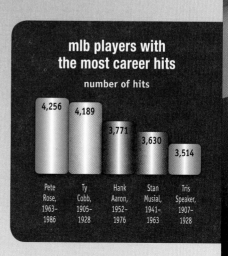

Pete Rose, 1963–1986	Ty Cobb, 1905–1928	Hank Aaron, 1952–1976	Stan Musial, 1941–1963	Tris Speaker, 1907–1928
4,256	4,189	3,771	3,630	3,514

mlb player with the highest batting average

Ty Cobb

Baseball legend Ty Cobb had a batting average of .367 during his 23-year career, and it has remained the highest average in MLB history for more than 80 years. Known as the "Georgia Peach," the American League outfielder set 90 different MLB records during his outstanding career. He won 12 batting titles, including 9 consecutive wins between 1907 and 1915. Cobb began his career with the Detroit Tigers in 1905, and later moved to the Philadelphia Athletics in 1927. Cobb was voted into the Baseball Hall of Fame in 1936 with 98.2 percent of the votes.

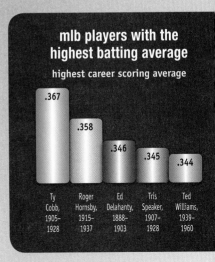

mlb players with the highest batting average

highest career scoring average

Ty Cobb, 1905–1928	Roger Hornsby, 1915–1937	Ed Delahanty, 1888–1903	Tris Speaker, 1907–1928	Ted Williams, 1939–1960
.367	.358	.346	.345	.344

mlb player with the most career runs

Rickey Henderson

During his 25 years in the majors, baseball great Rickey Henderson boasts the most career runs with 2,295. Henderson got his start with the Oakland Athletics in 1979, and went on to play for the Yankees, the Mets, the Mariners, the Red Sox, the Padres, the Dodgers, and the Angels. Henderson won a Gold Glove award in 1981, and the American League MVP award in 1989 and 1990. Henderson is also known as the "Man of Steal" because he holds the MLB record for most stolen bases in a career, with 1,406.

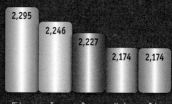

mlb players with the most career runs

number of career runs

Rickey Henderson, 1979–2003	Ty Cobb, 1905–1928	Barry Bonds, 1986–2007	Hank Aaron, 1954–1976	Babe Ruth, 1914–1935
2,295	2,246	2,227	2,174	2,174

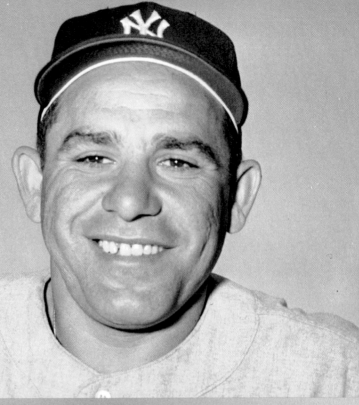

Yogi Berra

most mvp awards in the american league

Yogi Berra, Joe DiMaggio, Jimmie Foxx, Mickey Mantle & Alex Rodriguez

With three honors each, Yogi Berra, Joe DiMaggio, Jimmie Foxx, Mickey Mantle, and Alex Rodriguez all hold the record for the most Most Valuable Player awards during their professional careers. Berra, DiMaggio, Mantle, and Rodriguez were all New York Yankees. Foxx played for the Athletics, the Cubs, and the Phillies. The player with the biggest gap between wins was DiMaggio, who won his first award in 1939 and his last in 1947. Also nicknamed "Joltin' Joe" and the "Yankee Clipper," DiMaggio began playing in the Major Leagues in 1936. The following year, he led the league in home runs and runs scored. He was inducted into the Baseball Hall of Fame in 1955.

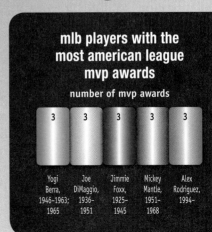

mlb players with the most american league mvp awards

number of mvp awards

Yogi Berra, 1946–1963; 1965	Joe DiMaggio, 1936– 1951	Jimmie Foxx, 1925– 1945	Mickey Mantle, 1951– 1968	Alex Rodriguez, 1994–
3	3	3	3	3

most mvp awards in the national league

Barry Bonds

San Francisco Giant Barry Bonds has earned seven Most Valuable Player awards for his amazing achievements in the National League. He received his first two MVP awards in 1990 and 1992 while playing for the Pittsburgh Pirates. The next five awards came while wearing the Giants uniform in 1993, 2001, 2002, 2003, and 2004. Bonds is the first player to win an MVP award three times in consecutive seasons. In fact, Bonds is the only baseball player in history to have won more than three MVP awards.

mlb players with the most national league mvp awards

number of mvp awards

Barry Bonds, 1986–2007	Roy Campanella, 1948–1957	Stan Musial, 1941–1963	Mike Schmidt, 1972–1989	Albert Pujols, 2001–
7	3	3	3	3

279

mlb team with the most world series wins

New York Yankees

Between 1923 and 2010, the New York Yankees were the World Series champions a record 27 times. The team picked up their latest win in October of 2009 when they beat the Philadelphia Phillies. The Yankees beat the Phillies four games to two to get their first win in nine years. Since their early days, the team has included some of baseball's greatest players, including Babe Ruth, Lou Gehrig, Yogi Berra, Joe DiMaggio, and Mickey Mantle.

mlb teams with the most world series wins

number of wins

NY Yankees	St. Louis Cardinals	Kansas City/ Philadelphia/ Oakland Athletics	Boston Red Sox	New York/ San Francisco Giants
27	11	9	7	6

mlb pitcher with the most cy young awards

Roger Clemens

Roger Clemens, a starting pitcher for the Houston Astros, earned a record seven Cy Young Awards during his career. He set a Major League record in April 1986, when he struck out 20 batters in one game. He later tied this record in September 1996. In September 2001, Clemens became the first Major League pitcher to win 20 of his first 21 decisions in one season. In June 2003, he became the first pitcher in more than a decade to win his 300th game. He also struck out his 4,000th batter that year.

mlb pitchers with the most cy young awards
number of cy young awards

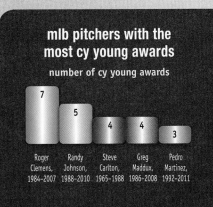

Roger Clemens, 1984–2007	Randy Johnson, 1988–2010	Steve Carlton, 1965–1988	Greg Maddux, 1986–2008	Pedro Martinez, 1992–2011
7	5	4	4	3

mlb player with the most at bats

Pete Rose

Pete Rose has stood behind the plate for 14,053 at bats—more than any other Major League player. Rose signed with the Cincinnati Reds after graduating from high school in 1963, and played second base. During his impressive career, Rose set several other records, including the most singles in the Major Leagues (3,315), most seasons with 600 or more at bats in the Major Leagues (17), most career doubles in the National League (746), and most career runs in the National League (2,165). He was also named World Series MVP, *Sports Illustrated*'s Sportsman of the Year, and the *Sporting News* Man of the Year.

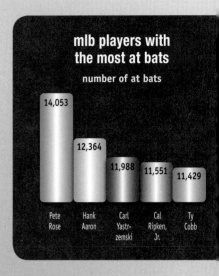

mlb players with the most at bats
number of at bats

Pete Rose	Hank Aaron	Carl Yastr-zemski	Cal Ripken, Jr.	Ty Cobb
14,053	12,364	11,988	11,551	11,429

mlb player with the most career RBIs

Hank Aaron

During his 23 years in the Major Leagues, right-handed Hank Aaron batted in an incredible 2,297 runs. Aaron began his professional career with the Indianapolis Clowns, a team in the Negro American League, in 1952. He was traded to the Milwaukee Braves in 1954 and won the National League batting championship with an average of .328. He was named the league's Most Valuable Player a year later when he led his team to a World Series victory. Aaron retired as a player in 1976 and was inducted into the Baseball Hall of Fame in 1982.

mlb players with the most career RBIs

number of runs batted in

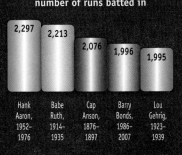

Hank Aaron, 1952–1976	Babe Ruth, 1914–1935	Cap Anson, 1876–1897	Barry Bonds, 1986–2007	Lou Gehrig, 1923–1939
2,297	2,213	2,076	1,996	1,995

283

mlb player with the most consecutive games played

Cal Ripken, Jr.

Baltimore Oriole Cal Ripken, Jr., played 2,632 consecutive games from May 30, 1982, to September 20, 1998. The right-handed third baseman also holds the record for the most consecutive innings played: 8,243. In June 1996, Ripken broke the world record for consecutive games with 2,216, surpassing Sachio Kinugasa of Japan. When he played as a shortstop, Ripken set Major League records for most home runs (345) and most extra-base hits (855) for his position. He started in the All-Star Game a record 19 times in a row.

mlb players with the most consecutive games played

number of consecutive games played

Cal Ripken, Jr., 1978–2001	Lou Gehrig, 1923–1939	Everett Scott, 1914–1925	Steve Garvey, 1968–1988	Miguel Tejada, 1997–
2,632	2,130	1,307	1,207	1,152

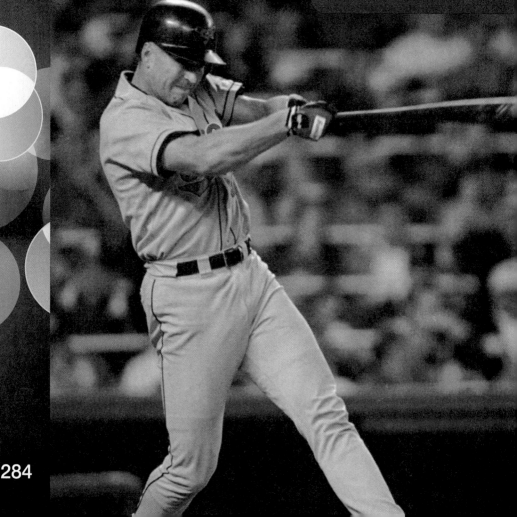

runner with the fastest mile

Hicham El Guerrouj

Moroccan runner Hicham El Guerrouj is super speedy—he ran a mile in just over 3 minutes and 43 seconds in July 1999 while racing in Rome. He also holds the record for the fastest mile in North America with a time just short of 3 minutes and 50 seconds. El Guerrouj is an Olympian with gold medals in the 1,500-meter and 5,000-meter races. With this accomplishment at the 2004 Athens games, he became the first runner in more than 75 years to win both races at the same Olympics. El Guerrouj returned to the Olympics in 2006 as a torchbearer in Torino, Italy.

runners with the fastest mile

time, in minutes and seconds

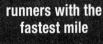

3:43.13	3:43.40	3:44.39	3:44.60	3:44.90
Hicham El Guerrouj, Morocco	Noah Ngeny, Kenya	Noureddine Morceli, Algeria	Hicham El Guerrouj, Morocco	Hicham El Guerrouj, Morocco

285

top-earning female tennis player

Serena Williams

Serena Williams has earned more than $46 million since she began playing professional tennis in 1995. During her amazing career, Williams has won 50 singles championships and 22 doubles championships, as well as three gold medals in the 2000, 2008, and 2012 Olympics. She has also won all four of the Grand Slam championships and holds 16 of those titles. Williams has won many impressive awards, including AP's Female Athlete of the Year, the BBC's Sports Personality of the Year, and two Espy Awards.

top-earning female tennis players

career earnings, in millions of US dollars

Serena Williams, 1995–	Venus Williams, 1994–	Maria Sharapova, 2001–	Kim Clijsters 1997–2012	Lindsay Davenport, 1993–2011
46.4	28.6	26.6	24.4	22.1

top-earning male tennis player

Roger Federer

Tennis great Roger Federer has earned $77.1 million since his career began in 1998. He has won 76 singles titles and 8 doubles titles, including 17 Grand Slams. His major victories include four Australian Opens, one French Open, six Wimbledon titles, and five US Opens. From February 2, 2004, to August 17, 2008, Federer was ranked first in the world for 237 consecutive weeks. He is also the only player in history to win five consecutive titles at two different Grand Slam tournaments (Wimbledon and US Open).

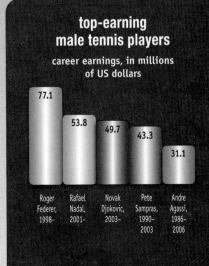

top-earning male tennis players

career earnings, in millions of US dollars

Roger Federer, 1998–	Rafael Nadal, 2001–	Novak Djokovic, 2003–	Pete Sampras, 1990–2003	Andre Agassi, 1986–2006
77.1	53.8	49.7	43.3	31.1

287

woman with the most grand slam singles titles

Margaret Court Smith

Margaret Court Smith won 24 Grand Slam singles titles between 1960 and 1975. She is the only woman ever to win the French, British, US, and Australian titles during one year in both the singles and doubles competitions. She was only the second woman to win all four singles titles in the same year. During her amazing career, she won a total of 64 Grand Slam championships—more than any other woman. Court was the world's top-seeded female player from 1962 to 1965, 1969 to 1970, and 1973. She was inducted into the International Tennis Hall of Fame in 1979.

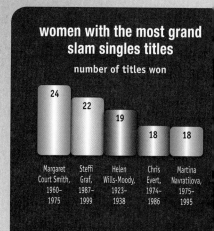

women with the most grand slam singles titles

number of titles won

Margaret Court Smith, 1960–1975	Steffi Graf, 1987–1999	Helen Wills-Moody, 1923–1938	Chris Evert, 1974–1986	Martina Navratilova, 1975–1995
24	22	19	18	18

man with the most grand slam singles titles

Roger Federer

Swiss tennis great Roger Federer has won a record 17 Grand Slam championship titles and earned more than $77 million since he turned pro in 1998. He has four Australian Open wins, one French Open win, seven Wimbledon wins, and five US Open wins. Federer is also one of only two players to win the Golden Slam—winning all four Grand Slam championships and an Olympic gold medal in the same year (2008). Federer achieved his 17th Grand Slam title when he defeated Andy Murray at the Wimbledon gentleman's final in 2012.

men with the most grand slam singles titles
number of titles won

Roger Federer, 2003–	Pete Sampras, 1990–2002	Roy Emerson, 1961–1967	Rafael Nadal, 2001–	Björn Borg, 1974–1981
17	14	12	12	11

highest-paid soccer player

David Beckham

David Beckham pulled in $50.6 million during 2013. He played for Paris Saint-Germain for five months, and donated his salary to a children's charity. About $44 million of his earnings came from endorsement deals, including Swedish underwear maker H&M. During his 21-year career, Beckham has played for Manchester United, Preston North End, Real Madrid, Los Angeles Galaxy, and Milan. The midfielder also played for the English National team, and was captain for 6 years. Beckham retired at the end of the French football season in May 2013.

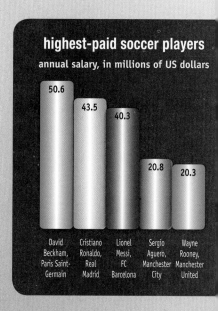

highest-paid soccer players
annual salary, in millions of US dollars

David Beckham, Paris Saint-Germain	50.6
Cristiano Ronaldo, Real Madrid	43.5
Lionel Messi, FC Barcelona	40.3
Sergio Aguero, Manchester City	20.8
Wayne Rooney, Manchester United	20.3

woman with the most CAPS

Kristine Lilly

With a total of 352, Kristine Lilly holds the world record for the most international games played, or CAPS. This is the highest number of CAPS in both the men's and women's international soccer organizations. She has a career total of 130 international goals—the second highest in the world. In 2004, Lilly scored her 100th international goal, becoming one of only five women to ever accomplish that feat. Lilly was named US Soccer's Female Athlete of the Year three times (1993, 2005, 2006). She retired in January 2011.

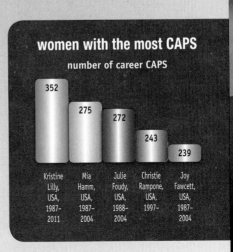

women with the most CAPS
number of career CAPS

Kristine Lilly, USA, 1987–2011	Mia Hamm, USA, 1987–2004	Julie Foudy, USA, 1988–2004	Christie Rampone, USA, 1997–	Joy Fawcett, USA, 1987–2004
352	275	272	243	239

man with the most CAPS

Ahmed Hassan

Ahmed Hassan, the captain for the Egyptian national soccer team and a midfielder for the Egyptian Premier League's Zamalek SC, has the most CAPS—or international games—with 184 appearances. He made his international debut in 1995. Hassan helped the National team win four CAF Africa Cup of Nations between 1998 and 2010, and was named the tournament's best player twice. He has also played in the Belgium Cup, the Turkish Cup, and the CAF Championship League. In 2010, Hassan was voted Best African-Based Player of the Year.

men with the most CAPS
number of career CAPS

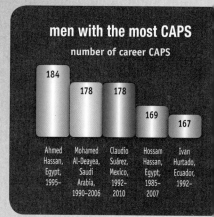

Ahmed Hassan, Egypt, 1995–	Mohamed Al-Deayea, Saudi Arabia, 1990–2006	Claudio Suárez, Mexico, 1992–2010	Hossam Hassan, Egypt, 1985–2007	Ivan Hurtado, Ecuador, 1992–
184	178	178	169	167

country with the most world cup points

Germany

Germany has accumulated a total of 33 points during World Cup soccer competition. A win is worth 4 points, runner-up is worth 3 points, third place is worth 2 points, and fourth place is worth 1 point. Germany won the World Cup three times between 1954 and 1990. Most recently, Germany earned 2 points for a third-place finish in 2010. The World Cup is organized by the Fédération Internationale de Football Association (FIFA) and is played every four years.

countries with the most world cup points

total number of points

Germany/ W. Germany, 1954–2006	Brazil, 1958–2002	Italy, 1934–2006	Argentina, 1978–1986	Uruguay, 1930–1950
33	30	25	14	10

driver with the most formula one wins

Michael Schumacher

Race-car driver Michael Schumacher won 91 Formula One races in his professional career, which began in 1991. Out of the 250 races he competed in, he reached the podium 154 times. In 2002, Schumacher became the only Formula One driver to have a podium finish in each race in which he competed that season. He won seven world championships between 1994 and 2004. Schumacher, who was born in Germany, began his career with Benetton but later switched to Ferrari. He retired from racing in 2006.

drivers with the most formula one wins
number of wins

Michael Schumacher	Alain Prost	Ayrton Senna	Fernando Alonso	Nigel Mansell
91	51	41	32	31

driver with the fastest daytona 500 win

Buddy Baker

Race-car legend Buddy Baker dominated the competition at the 1980 Daytona 500 with an average speed of over 177 miles (285 km) per hour. It was the first Daytona 500 race run in under three hours. Baker had a history of speed before this race—he became the first driver to race more than 200 miles (322 km) per hour on a closed course in 1970. During his amazing career, Baker competed in 688 Winston Cup races—he won 19 of them and finished in the top five in 198 others. He also won more than $3.6 million. He was inducted into the International Motorsports Hall of Fame in 1997.

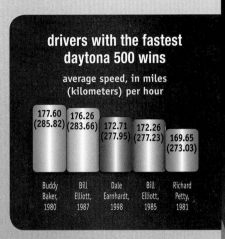

drivers with the fastest daytona 500 wins

average speed, in miles (kilometers) per hour

177.60 (285.82)	176.26 (283.66)	172.71 (277.95)	172.26 (277.23)	169.65 (273.03)
Buddy Baker, 1980	Bill Elliott, 1987	Dale Earnhardt, 1998	Bill Elliott, 1985	Richard Petty, 1981

driver with the most consecutive sprint cup championships

Jimmie Johnson

Jimmie Johnson has won five consecutive Sprint Cup Championships between 2006 and 2010. With his 54 series wins, he is ranked 10th in career victories. During his career, Johnson has also had 138 top-five finishes and 208 top-ten finishes. He has been named Driver of the Year four times, which is a record he holds with teammate Jeff Gordon. Johnson joined the Hendrick Motorsports team in 2002, and drives a Chevrolet owned by Gordon. In addition to his Sprint Cup victories, Johnson has won the Daytona 500 one time and the Coca-Cola 500 and the All State 400 three times each.

drivers with the most consecutive sprint cup championships

consecutive wins

Jimmie Johnson, 2006–2010	Cale Yarborough, 1976–1978	Jeff Gordon, 1997–1998	Dale Earnhardt, 1993–1994	Darrell Waltrip, 1981–1982
5	3	2	2	2

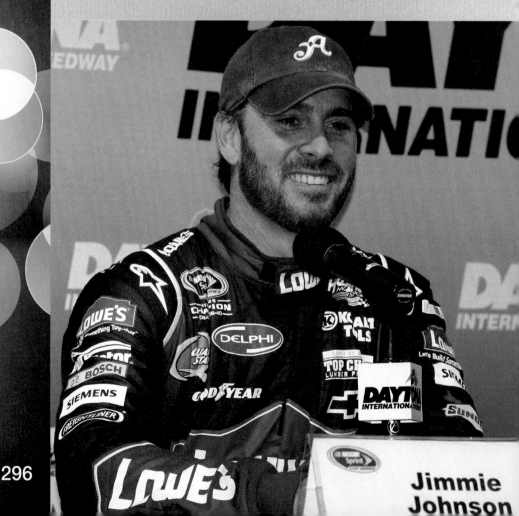

Jimmie Johnson

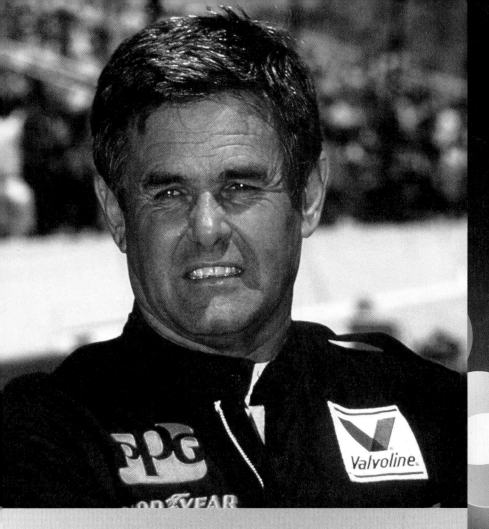

indy 500 career lap leader

Al Unser, Sr.

Racing legend Al Unser has led more race laps than any other driver in Indy 500 history with 644. During his career, Unser had 27 Indy 500 starts, led for 11 of them, and won 4. Racing from 1965 until 1993, he claimed his first Indy victory in 1970 with an average speed of 155.7 miles (250.5 km) per hour. He also won the following year from a fifth-place starting position. Unser picked up his third Indy win in 1978 with a nine-second lead. His last victory came in 1987 when he moved from the 20th position to the front of the pack, finishing with an average speed of 162.1 miles per hour (260.8 km/h).

indy 500 career lap leaders
career indy 500 laps led

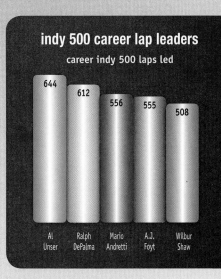

Al Unser	Ralph DePalma	Mario Andretti	A.J. Foyt	Wilbur Shaw
644	612	556	555	508

highest-paid NASCAR driver

Dale Earnhardt, Jr.

In 2012, NASCAR driver Dale Earnhardt, Jr. won $25.9 million. This total includes race winnings, as well as income earned for several endorsements including Wrangler, Chevrolet, and Dollar General. During his career, he has won more than $100 million. Earnhardt drives the number 88 Chevy Impala for Hendrick Motors in the NASCAR Sprint Cup Series. He's competed in more than 450 NASCAR Sprint Cup races and 120 NASCAR Nationwide Series races during his 16-year career. Earnhardt, Jr. has 19 career wins, and 108 top-five finishes. He won the Daytona 500 in 2004, and the Busch Series Championship in 1998 and 1999.

highest-paid NASCAR drivers

earnings in 2012, in millions of US dollars

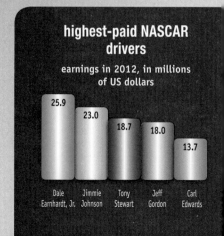

Dale Earnhardt, Jr.	Jimmie Johnson	Tony Stewart	Jeff Gordon	Carl Edwards
25.9	23.0	18.7	18.0	13.7

rider with the most superbike race points

Max Biaggi

Italian rider Max Biaggi scored the most Superbike race points in 2012 with 358. Finishing half a point ahead of his nearest opponent, this is the smallest margin of victory ever in the sport. As part of the Aprilia Alitalia team, he competed in 27 races and earned five wins and 11 podium finishes. Biaggi also won the World Superbike Championship with a total of 451 race points in 2010. Before racing Superbikes, he had a successful career racing 250cc and 500cc bikes. Biaggi retired from racing at the end of the 2012 season and now works as a racing commentator for an Italian TV network. During his six-year career, Biaggi competed in 155 races with 21 wins and 70 podium finishes.

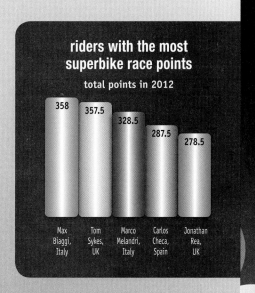

riders with the most superbike race points

total points in 2012

Max Biaggi, Italy	Tom Sykes, UK	Marco Melandri, Italy	Carlos Checa, Spain	Jonathan Rea, UK
358	357.5	328.5	287.5	278.5

rider with the most motocross world titles

Stefan Everts

Stefan Everts is the king of motocross with a total of ten world titles. He won twice on a 500cc bike, seven more times on a 250cc bike, and once on a 125cc bike. During his 18-year career, he had 101 Grand Prix victories. Everts was named Belgium Sportsman of the Year five times. He retired after his final world title in 2006 and is now a consultant and coach for the riders who compete for the KTM racing team.

riders with the most motocross world titles
number of wins

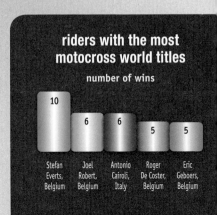

Stefan Everts, Belgium	Joel Robert, Belgium	Antonio Cairoli, Italy	Roger De Coster, Belgium	Eric Geboers, Belgium
10	6	6	5	5

jockey with the most triple crown wins

Eddie Arcaro

Between 1938 and 1961, jockey Eddie Arcaro won a total of 17 Triple Crown races. Nicknamed "the Master," Arcaro won the Kentucky Derby five times, the Preakness six times, and the Belmont six times. He holds the record for the most Preakness wins, and is tied for the most Kentucky Derby and Belmont wins. He was also horse racing's top money winner six times between 1940 and 1955. During his career, Arcaro competed in 24,092 races and won 4,779 of them.

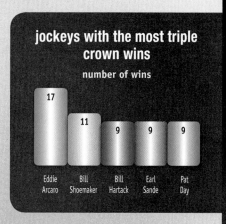

jockeys with the most triple crown wins

number of wins

Eddie Arcaro	Bill Shoemaker	Bill Hartack	Earl Sande	Pat Day
17	11	9	9	9

nhl team with the most stanley cup wins

Montreal Canadiens

The Montreal Canadiens won an amazing 24 Stanley Cup victories between 1916 and 1993. That's almost one-quarter of all the Stanley Cup championships ever played. The team plays at Montreal's Molson Centre. The Canadiens were created in December 1909 by J. Ambrose O'Brien to play for the National Hockey Association (NHA). They eventually made the transition into the National Hockey League. Over the years, the Canadiens have included such great players as Maurice Richard, George Hainsworth, Jacques Lemaire, Saku Koivu, and Emile Bouchard.

nhl teams with the most stanley cup wins

number of stanley cup wins

Montreal Canadiens	Toronto Maple Leafs	Detroit Red Wings	Boston Bruins	Edmonton Oilers
24	13	11	6	5

nhl player with the most career points

Wayne Gretzky

Wayne Gretzky scored an unbelievable 2,857 points and 894 goals during his 20-year career. Gretzky was the first person in the NHL to average more than two points per game. Many people consider Canadian-born Gretzky to be the greatest player in the history of the National Hockey League. In fact, he is called "The Great One." He officially retired from the sport in 1999 and was inducted into the Hockey Hall of Fame that same year. After his final game, the NHL retired his jersey number (99). In 2005, Gretzky became the head coach of the Phoenix Coyotes.

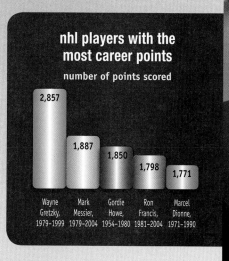

nhl players with the most career points

number of points scored

Wayne Gretzky, 1979–1999	2,857
Mark Messier, 1979–2004	1,887
Gordie Howe, 1954–1980	1,850
Ron Francis, 1981–2004	1,798
Marcel Dionne, 1971–1990	1,771

nhl goalie with the most career wins

Martin Brodeur

Not much gets by goalie Martin Brodeur—he's won 669 games since he was drafted by the New Jersey Devils in 1990. Still playing with the Devils, Brodeur has helped the team win three Stanley Cup championships. He is also the only goalie in NHL history to complete seven seasons with 40 or more wins. Brodeur has been an NHL All-Star ten times. He has received the Vezina Trophy four times and the Jennings Trophy five times. He also ranks first in the league in regular-season shutouts.

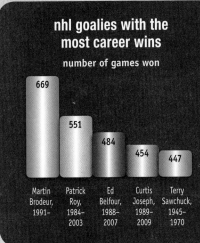

nhl goalies with the most career wins

number of games won

Martin Brodeur, 1991–	Patrick Roy, 1984–2003	Ed Belfour, 1988–2007	Curtis Joseph, 1989–2009	Terry Sawchuck, 1945–1970
669	551	484	454	447

nhl player with the most power play goals

Dave Andreychuk

Dave Andreychuk has scored more power play goals than any other player in NHL history with 274. A power play occurs when one team has all five players on the ice, and the other team has at least one player in the penalty box. The full-strength team has a huge advantage to score with the extra player on the ice. Andreychuk was in the NHL from 1982 to 2006, and played for the Buffalo Sabres, the Toronto Maple Leafs, the New Jersey Devils, the Boston Bruins, the Colorado Avalanche, and the Tampa Bay Lightning. With a total of 1,338 points, he is one of the highest-scoring left wings in NHL history.

nhl players with the most power play goals

power play goals

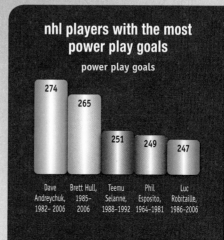

Dave Andreychuk, 1982–2006	Brett Hull, 1985–2006	Teemu Selanne, 1988–1992	Phil Esposito, 1964–1981	Luc Robitaille, 1986–2006
274	265	251	249	247

nhl player with the most overtime winning goals

Jaromir Jagr

Jaromir Jagr works well under pressure—he has 17 overtime winning goals during his 23-year NHL career. He also holds the record for the most points by a right wing with 149. He was the fifth overall draft pick in 1990. Currently a Boston Bruin, Jagr has also played for the Pittsburgh Penguins, the Washington Capitals, the New York Rangers, the Philadelphia Flyers, and the Dallas Stars. He also has two Olympic medals, and—in 1991 and 1992—he helped the Penguins win the Stanley Cup.

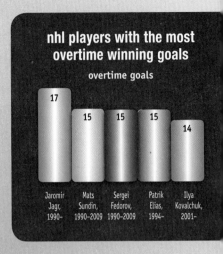

nhl players with the most overtime winning goals

overtime goals

Jaromir Jagr, 1990–	Mats Sundin, 1990–2009	Sergei Fedorov, 1990–2009	Patrik Elias, 1994–	Ilya Kovalchuk, 2001–
17	15	15	15	14

highest-paid hockey player

Sidney Crosby

In 2012, Sidney Crosby earned $12.7 million through his NHL salary and endorsements. The Pittsburgh Penguins pay Crosby $8.7 million per year, and he banked another $4 million in endorsements for Reebok, Gatorade, and Bell. The Canadian center was the first overall draft pick in 2005, and was the captain of the gold-medal-winning Team Canada at the 2010 Olympic Games. He holds several NHL records, which include being the youngest player voted to the starting lineup in an All-Star Game, and the youngest player to reach 200 career points.

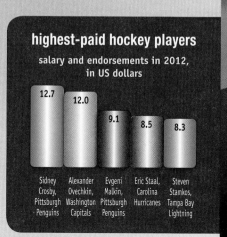

highest-paid hockey players
salary and endorsements in 2012, in US dollars

12.7	12.0	9.1	8.5	8.3
Sidney Crosby, Pittsburgh Penguins	Alexander Ovechkin, Washington Capitals	Evgeni Malkin, Pittsburgh Penguins	Eric Staal, Carolina Hurricanes	Steven Stamkos, Tampa Bay Lightning

Index

Photo Credits

Throughout: abstract background, iStockphoto

CONTENTS:
bottom right: Christopher Polk/Getty Images; bottom left: Scott Boehm/AP Photo; middle right: Columbia Pictures/Everett Collection.

SCIENCE & TECHNOLOGY:
4 bottom: Mike Kemp/Getty Images (RF); 5 bottom: iStockphoto; 5 top: Iain Masterton/Alamy; 6 top left: Lionel Bonaventure/AFP/Getty Images/Newscom; 6 bottom right: Luc Novovitch/Alamy; 7 bottom: iStockphoto; 7 top: courtesy of Alton Towers Resort; 8 top: Emily Teresa; 9 bottom: Provided by Nintendo/MCT/Newscom; 10 top: Nintendo; 11 bottom: Eric Carr/Alamy; 12 bottom: Alex Segr/Alamy; 13 bottom: Alex Segr/Alamy; 14 top: Tripplaar Kristoffer/SIPA/Newscom; 15 bottom: Universal Music Group; 16 center left: Thomas Coex/AFP/Getty Images; 16 center right: Kim Jae-Hwan/AFP/Getty Images; 16 top: OZAN KOSE/AFP/Getty Images; 17 center left: Zynga; 17 bottom right: Zygna; 18 left: razorpi/Alamy; 19 bottom: Theo Wargo/2012 Getty Images; 20 top: Screenshot/Alamy; 21 bottom: incamerastock/Alamy; 22 bottom: Charles Krupa/AP Images; 23 top: Mary Evans/Studio Ghibli Ronald Grant/Everett Collection; 24 bottom: Shutterstock; 25 top: Zhudifeng/Dreamstime; 26 top: Bloomberg via Getty Images; 27 bottom: Davide Illini/iStockphoto; 28 top: incamerastock/Alamy; 29 bottom: Ian Dagnall/Alamy; 30 bottom: Jeffrey Blackler/Alamy; 31 top: Greenland/Dreamstime; 32 bottom: Laszlo Halasi/Shutterstock; 33 top: AFP/Getty Images; 34 top: BIGFOOT 4x4, Inc, 2011; 35 bottom: Shelley Mays/AP Photo; 36 top: Getty Images; 37 bottom: courtesy of Marine Turbine Technologies, Inc.; 38 bottom: Fabrice Coffrini/AFP/Getty Images/Newscom; 39 top: C. David LaBianca/Sikokorsky; 40 top: Danjaq/Eon/UA/The Kobal Collection; 41 bottom: NASA; 42 bottom: Mike Derer/AP Photo; 43 top: Courtesy of Cedar Point; 44 top: Ferrari World, Abu Dhabi; 45 bottom: Songquan Deng/Shutterstock; 46: Kamran Jebreili/AP Photo; 47 top: Focus/Alamy; 48 top: Korean Central News Agency via Korea News Service/AP Photo; 49 bottom: Barry Williams/Getty Images; 50 bottom: Imaginechina/AP Images; 51 top: Steve Allen/Getty Images.

MONEY:
52 bottom: Claire Quinn, McDonald's/AP Photo; 53 top: Alain Benainous/Gamma-Rapho/Getty Images; 53 bottom: iStockphoto; 54 top: Clive Brunskill/Getty Images; 54 bottom: Ben Hider/Getty Images; 55 top: Will Oliver/AFP/Getty Images; 55 bottom: Jonathan Hordle/Rex Features/AP Photo; 56 bottom: President Wilson Hotel, Geneva; 57 top: Timothy A. Clary/AFP/Getty Images; 58 bottom: Chris Pizzello/AP Photo; 59 top: Deck Uli/DPA/ABACA/Newscom; 60 top: SCP Auctions/AP Photo; 61 bottom: Cal Sport Media/AP Images; 62 bottom: The Washington Post/Getty Images; 63 top: Brian Babineau/

NHLI/Getty Images; 64 top: Michael Regan/Getty Images; 65 bottom: Ralph Freso/Getty Images; 66 bottom: Brian Kimball/KimballStock; 67 top: Bruce Glassman; 68 top: Robert Convery/Alamy; 69 bottom: Dale de la Rey/Bloomberg via Getty Images.

POP CULTURE:
70: Jeff Vespa/WireImage/Getty Images; 71 top: Walt Disney/Photofest; 71 bottom: Paul Buck/EPA/Newscom; 72 top right: Newscom; 72 bottom: Walt Disney Studios Motion Pictures/Photofest; 73 top right: Fox Television/Photofest; 73 bottom: Torsten Blackwood/AFP/Getty Images; 74 top: Robin Marchant/Getty Images; 75 bottom: Barry King/Getty Images; 76 bottom: Charles Sykes/AP Images; 77 top: Reed Saxon/AP Photo; 78 bottom: Jason Merritt/Getty Images; 79 top: NBC Sports Group; 80 top: Jeff Kravitz/FilmMagic/Getty Images; 81 bottom: Dimitrios Kambouris/WireImage/Getty Images; 82 top: Ray Amati/NBAE/Getty Images; 83 bottom: Mark J. Terrill/AP Photo; 84 top: Evan Agostini/AP Photo; 85 bottom: Kevork Djansezian/AP Photo; 86 top: Matt Sayles/AP Photo; 87 bottom: Jason Merritt/Getty Images; 88 bottom: Mike Marsland/WireImage/Getty Images; 89 top: Universal Pictures/Photofest; 90 bottom: ZUMA Press/Newscom; 91 top: Columbia Pictures/Everett Collection; 92 bottom: Twentieth Century Fox Film Corporation/Photofest; 93 top: Nick Ut/AP Photo; 94 bottom: Dave M. Benett/WireImage/Getty Images; 95 top: Jason Merritt/Getty Images; 96 top: g90/g90/ZUMA Press/Newscom; 97 bottom: Stephen Vaughan/Buena Vista Pictures/Photofest; 98 bottom: Courtesy Everett Collection; 99 top: Murray Close/ Lionsgate/Everett Collection; 100 top: Ben Glass/Warner Bros/Regency/Canal+/The Kobal Collection; 101 bottom: AP Photo; 102 top: Leon Neal/Getty Images; 103 bottom: SH5 WENN Photos/Newscom; 104 top: George Pimentel/WireImage/Getty Images; 105 bottom: Bennett Raglin/WireImage/Getty Images; 106 bottom: Bill Frakes/Getty Images; 107 top: Christopher Polk/Getty Images; 108 top: Malte Christians/Zuma Press; 109 bottom: Christopher Polk/Getty Images; 110 top: Ethan Miller/Getty Images; 111 bottom: David Buchan/Getty Images; 112 bottom: Britta Pedersen/picture alliance/dpa/Newscom; 113 top: Evan Agostin/AP Photo; 114 bottom: Larry Marano/Getty Images; 115 top: Mark Humphrey/AP Photo; 116 top: David Karp/AP Photo; 117 bottom: Greg Wood/AFP/Getty Images.

NATURE:
118 bottom: yuriy kulik/Shutterstock; 119 bottom: NASA; 120 top: Francois Lenoir/Reuters; 120 bottom right: iStockphoto; 121 top left: Laurence Dutton/Getty Images; 121 bottom: Courtesy Ted Scambos and Rob Bauer/NSIDC; 122 bottom: Borsheim's Jewelry Store/AP Photo; 123 top: Pichugin Dmitry/Shutterstock; 124 bottom: Eye Ubiquitous/Alamy; 125 top: Galyna Andrushko/Shutterstock; 126 top: Baloncici/Dreamstime; 127 bottom: Vladislav Turchenko/Dreamstime; 128 top:

Read for the World Record!

WWW.SCHOLASTIC.COM/SUMMER

KIDS ANSWERED THE CHALLENGE!

Kids from every state in the U.S. and 31 countries around the world participated in the Scholastic Summer Challenge™ to set a new world record for summer reading!

As part of the Scholastic Summer Challenge, students were united in an attempt to read as many minutes as possible between May 6 and September 6, 2013 to help set a new Read for the World Record.

CONGRATULATIONS TO ALL STUDENTS WHO HELPED SET THE RECORD!

Total minutes read from
May 6 to September 6, 2013: **176,438,473**

Millions of Reading Minutes

2012	A New World Record! 176,438,473
2012	95,859,491
2011	64,213,141
2010	52,710,386
2009	35,846,094

0 10 20 30 40 50 60 70 80 90 100 110 120 130 140 150 160 170 180 190 200

Read for the World Record!

CHECK OUT THESE COOL FACTS:

TOP 20 STATES WITH THE MOST MINUTES READ:

1.	Texas	46,351,247	11.	Virginia	3,073,712
2.	Florida	40,204,567	12.	South Carolina	2,908,845
3.	North Carolina	10,357,993	13.	Massachusetts	2,619,040
4.	New York	6,820,343	14.	Georgia	2,035,315
5.	New Jersey	5,557,675	15.	Utah	1,975,038
6.	Nebraska	4,105,264	16.	Ohio	1,840,083
7.	California	4,011,561	17.	Michigan	1,715,024
8.	Pennsylvania	3,849,486	18.	Kentucky	1,633,517
9.	Louisiana	3,507,120	19.	Wisconsin	1,587,749
10.	Illinois	3,097,845	20.	Washington	1,143,499

STATES WITH THE MOST MINUTES READ

Did your state make the top 20?

BIGGEST STATE!

Texas led the nation in minutes read this summer with 46,351,247. That's 30 million minutes more than the state entered last year! The Aldine School District in Houston had five schools in the top 20 and overall schools in the district entered more than 30 million minutes.

STUDENTS FROM AROUND THE WORLD PARTICIPATED!

Two international schools read enough minutes to rank in the top 100 worldwide: Our Lady of Mercy School, Rio de Janeiro, Brazil (#22); Seoul Foreign School, Seoul, South Korea (#41). Schools from 31 countries added minutes to the new world record, including:

Brazil	China	Netherland	South Korea	
Canada	Dubai	Antilles	Taiwan	United Kingdom
Cayman Islands	Japan	Nicaragua	Thailand	Venezuela

Number of participating schools: **4,287**

Total number of students: **133,289**

242 schools logged 100,000 minutes or more.

THE TOP SUMMER READING SCHOOL!

Top honor in the 2013 Scholastic Summer Challenge goes to Jackson Elementary School in McAllen, TX, whose students read **6,333,482** minutes toward the Read for the World Record!

Members of Jackson Elementary School with their minutes.

THE REST OF THE TOP 20 SUMMER READING SCHOOLS!

These schools round out the top 20 list and are recognized for their outstanding contribution toward setting the new world record:

Sun Valley Elementary School	Monroe, NC	6,042,663
Dovalina Elementary School	Laredo, TX	5,359,066
Liberty Park Elementary School	Greenacres, FL	4,206,222
Hill Intermediate School	Houston, TX	3,039,434
St. Aloysius School	Baton Rouge, LA	2,933,169
Odom Elementary School	Houston, TX	2,771,182
Hunters Creek Elementary School	Orlando, FL	2,565,217
Flora Ridge Elementary School	Kissimmee, FL	2,548,754
Timber Trace Elementary School	Palm Beach Gardens, FL	2,288,345
Reedy Creek Elementary School	Kissimmee, FL	2,238,484
Rayford Road Intermediate School	Humble, TX	2,183,113
Oakridge Middle School	Clover, SC	2,122,819
Worsham Elementary School	Houston, TX	1,898,592
Newell Elementary School	Allentown, NJ	1,885,364
Coral Reef Elementary School	Lake Worth, FL	1,673,656
Stuart Public Schools	Stuart, NE	1,639,619
Raymond Academy	Houston, TX	1,623,279
Thompson Elementary School	Houston, TX	1,604,302
Riverview Elementary School	Saratoga Springs, UT	1,495,565

Read for the World Record!

THE BEST OF THE REST SPECIAL BONUS SECTION!

These schools all earned top state school honors by reading more than all the schools in their state.

School	Location	School	Location
Old Harbor School	Old Harbor, AK	Belgrade Intermediate School	Belgrade, MT
Valley Intermediate School	Pelham, AL	Sun Valley Elementary School	Monroe, NC
Eastside Elementary School	Cabot, AR	Jefferson Elementary School	Fargo, ND
Summit School of Ahwatukee	Phoenix, AZ	Stuart Public Schools	Stuart, NE
Don Juan Avila Elementary School	Aliso Viejo, CA	Broken Ground Elementary School	Concord, NH
Prospect Ridge Academy	Broomfield, CO	Newell Elementary School	Allentown, NJ
Huckleberry Elementary School	Brookfield, CT	Bandelier Elementary School	Albuquerque, NM
Dupont Park School	Washington, DC	Dooley Elementary School	Henderson, NV
St. Anne's Episcopal School	Middletown, DE	Village Elementary School	Hilton, NY
Liberty Park Elementary School	Greenacres, FL	Mason Middle School	Mason, OH
Savannah Country Day School	Savannah, GA	Northeast Elementary School	Owasso, OK
Laie Elementary School	Laie, HI	Holy Cross Area School	Portland, OR
Clayton Ridge Elementary School	Guttenberg, IA	Gettysburg Area Middle School	Gettysburg, PA
Peregrine Elementary School	Meridian, ID	Countryside Children's Center	Portsmouth, RI
Enders - Salk Elementary School	Schaumburg, IL	Oakridge Middle School	Clover, SC
Promise Road Elementary School	Noblesville, IN	Jefferson Elementary School	Watertown, SD
Sacred Heart of Jesus School	Shawnee, KS	Crosswind Elementary School	Collierville, TN
Veterans Park Elementary School	Lexington, KY	Jackson Elementary School	McAllen, TX
St. Aloysius School	Baton Rouge, LA	Riverview Elementary School	Saratoga Springs, UT
South River Elementary School	Marshfield, MA	Ashburn Elementary School	Ashburn, VA
Glenallan Elementary School	Silver Spring, MD	Irasburg Village School	Irasburg, VT
Telstar Middle School	Bethel, ME	Highlands Elementary School	Renton, WA
Rawsonville Elementary School	Ypsilanti, MI	Hillcrest Elementary School	Chippewa Falls, WI
Emmet D. Williams Elem. School	Shoreview, MN	St. Francis Central	
Chillicothe Middle School	Chillicothe, MO	Catholic School	Morgantown, WV
Annunciation Catholic School	Columbus, MS	Pronghorn Elementary School	Gillette, WY

SCHOLASTIC
SUMMER
CHALLENGE
★ ★ ★ ★

WWW.SCHOLASTIC.COM/SUMMER